WORKING WI ...   ...HROUGH
S...

BASIC TEXTS IN COUNSELLING AND PSYCHOTHERAPY

Series editor: Stephen Frosh

This series introduces readers to the theory and practice of counselling and psychotherapy across a wide range of topic areas. The books appeal to anyone wishing to use counselling and psychotherapeutic skills and are particularly relevant to workers in health, education, social work and related settings. The books are unusual in being rooted in psychodynamic and systemic ideas, yet being written at an accessible, readable and introductory level. Each text offers theoretical background and guidance for practice, with creative use of clinical examples.

Published

Jenny Altschuler
WORKING WITH CHRONIC ILLNESS

Bill Barnes, Sheila Ernst and Keith Hyde
AN INTRODUCTION TO GROUPWORK

Stephen Briggs
WORKING WITH ADOLESCENTS

Alex Coren
SHORT-TERM PSYCHOTHERAPY

Emilia Dowling and Gill Gorell Barnes
WORKING WITH CHILDREN AND PARENTS THROUGH SEPARATION AND DIVORCE

Loretta Franklin
AN INTRODUCTION TO WORKPLACE COUNSELLING

Gill Gorell Barnes
FAMILY THERAPY IN CHANGING TIMES 2nd Edition

Sally Modyes
COUNSELLING ADULTS WITH LEARNING DISABLITIES

Ravi Rana
COUNSELLING STUDENTS

Tricia Scott
INTEGRATIVE PSYCHOTHERAPY IN HEALTHCARE

Geraldine Shipton
WORKING WITH EATING DISORDERS

Laurence Spurling
AN INTRODUCTION TO PSYCHODYNAMIC COUNSELLING

Paul Terry
WORKING WITH THE ELDERLY AND THEIR CARERS

Jan Wiener and Mannie Sher
COUNSELLING AND PSYCHOTHERAPY IN PRIMARY HEALTH CARE

Shula Wilson
COUNSELLING ADULTS WITH LEARNING DISABILITIES

Invitation to authors

The Series Editor welcomes proposals for new books within the Basic Texts in Counselling and Psychotherapy series. These should be sent to Stephen Frosh at the School of Psychology, Birkbeck College, Malet Street, London, WC1E 7HX (e-mail s.frosh@bbk.ac.uk)

**Basic Texts in Counselling and Psychotherapy
Series Standing Order ISBN 0–333–69330–2**
(outside North America only)

You can receive future titles in this series as they are published by placing a standing order. Please contact your bookseller or, in the case of difficulty, write to us at the address below with your name and address, the title of the series and the ISBN quoted above.

Customer Services Department, Macmillan Distribution Ltd
Houndmills, Basingstoke, Hampshire RG21 6XS, England

WORKING WITH CHILDREN AND PARENTS THROUGH SEPARATION AND DIVORCE

THE CHANGING LIVES OF CHILDREN

EMILIA DOWLING

AND

GILL GORELL BARNES

Published by
PALGRAVE MACMILLAN
Houndmills, Basingstoke, Hampshire RG21 6XS and
175 Fifth Avenue, New York, N. Y. 10010
Companies and representatives throughout the world

PALGRAVE MACMILLAN is the global academic imprint of the Palgrave
Macmillan division of St. Martin's Press, LLC and of Palgrave Macmillan Ltd.
Macmillan® is a registered trademark in the United States, United Kingdom
and other countries. Palgrave is a registered trademark in the European
Union and other countries.

ISBN 0–333–71952–2

This book is printed on paper suitable for recycling and
made from fully managed and sustained forest sources.

A catalogue record for this book is available from the British Library.

Transferred to digital printing 2002

Printed and bound in Great Britain by
Antony Rowe Ltd, Chippenham and Eastbourne

Learning   ces

FOR OUR FAMILIES

CONTENTS

ACKNOWLEDGEMENTS

First and foremost we would like to express our gratitude to the families we have worked with, from whom we have learned so much. We would like to thank the Tavistock Clinic, in particular colleagues in the family systems team and those postgraduate students who were part of the divorce project. We would also like to thank colleagues in general practice, and the schools we have worked with over the years.

In addition our thanks go to Professor Stephen Frosh, series editor, for his encouragement and feedback throughout the writing process, to Debi Schifreen for her patient preparation of the typescript and to Josephine Campbell and John Dowling for their generous help with proofreading.

EMILIA DOWLING
GILL GORELL BARNES

Introduction

The Changing Lives of Children: Working with Families through Separation and Divorce

Over the last two decades family life in westernised countries has undergone fundamental and dramatic changes. The increase in the number of divorces, single parents and reconstituted families has resulted in a significant number of children growing up in different family configurations from that of the traditional nuclear family. According to recent research (Rodgers and Pryor, 1998, p. 4) 'On recent trends it is estimated that 19% of children born to married couples will experience parental divorce by the age of ten and 28% by age sixteen. However, these figures may underestimate the rate of family dissolution, since they do not include the separation of cohabiting parents.'

These social changes have not only affected the families involved but have taken centrestage in the political arena. Single parents, for example, have been blamed for unruly children, and in the UK the child support agency was created to follow up fathers, ostensibly to ensure that they face up to their financial responsibilities but covertly to remind them of their parental commitment. Divorce and separation have been seen as both liberating for adults, particularly for women, and as disastrous for children. The picture that emerges is confusing: is it better for children to live with constantly warring parents or to suffer the effects (psychological, social and financial) of their parents' divorce? In the UK, legislation stressing the notion of *parental responsibility* (Children Act, 1989) has fundamentally changed the emphasis from the *rights* of parents to the *best interests* of the children, from *access* to *contact*, and from *rights* to *responsibility*. Children's needs have moved to the foreground.

In the context of all these changes, professionals in health, education and social services are increasingly faced with the aftermath of family break-up. The manifestations in terms of emotional and behavioural difficulties in children, depression and stress in adults and ongoing conflict which may have been the reason for the separation in the first place, are not usually met by increased resources in the professional community.

This book represents an attempt to examine what we have learned from our work in a National Health Service setting in the UK, providing a therapeutic service to families during and after separation and divorce. We are interested in the application of our findings in the clinical context to the 'front-line' primary care and education settings, where professionals are faced with the difficulties children and families experience as a result of this increasingly common life transition. While we write from the perspective of workers based in a large city in one part of Europe, the families that we have worked with come from across the globe, Africa, North and South America, India and East Asia as well as Europe (see Chapter 3). Our findings on children's stress in the context of parental break-up therefore has a wider application than to the UK itself. Although the structures for bringing up children differ around the world, a parental decision to live apart (in Westernised cultures at least) carries powerful common reverberations for children, as research from Australia, New Zealand and the United States has shown.

In the last 20 years research in the social sciences has been concerned with the effects of changes in family structure on the psychological functioning of children and adults, focusing in particular on single versus two-parent households. In the 1970s and early 1980s, high divorce rates and an increase in the number of single-parent families were seen by social scientists as an indication that unhappy couples no longer felt obliged to stay together, oppressed women were able to free themselves from marital relationships in which they felt trapped and children would be free from the burden of ongoing parental conflict. These changes tended to be interpreted more as a sign of social evolution than social disorganisation. Therefore, social scientists at that time tended to regard alternative family structures as equally viable environments for child and adult development (Simons, 1996).

During the 1980s, further research studies became available showing the negative effects of divorce, particularly on children. For example, a variety of studies (Amato and Keith, 1993; McLanahan and Booth, 1989; McLanahan and Sandefeur, 1994) reported that children in single-parent families:

- had more difficulties in school;
- were more sexually active;
- suffered higher rates of depression; and
- were more likely to exhibit delinquent behaviour and substance abuse.

Some of these findings have been corroborated in the UK by Cockett and Tripp (1994).

This evidence has made most researchers aware of, and concerned with, the potential negative effects of divorce on children's emotional and psychological development. Some researchers, therefore, have taken the view that changes in family structure are a major contributing factor to social problems, while others maintain that too much emphasis is placed on family structure and it is other factors such us poverty and conflict which are more likely to affect psychological well-being. This latter viewpoint would include some feminists who would see the more negative interpretation of alternative family structures as an attempt to threaten and undermine the status of women (Allen, 1993; Stacey, 1993). A developmental perspective suggests that 'parental divorce represents a significant risk factor for child developmental problems'. Simons et al. (1996, p. 7). Other researchers stress the complex factors that impinge on families before, during and after separation which indicate that divorce as a *process* rather than as a *single event* needs to be examined (Rodgers and Pryor, 1998).

Given that it is unlikely that the social trend towards increasing variety in family structures will be reversed, this book is concerned with examining the conditions which can help children and families to minimise the harmful effects of family disruption and to promote psychological well-being in children and appropriate parenting skills in adults. The work described in this book and our wish to make our experience and knowledge from working with a clinical sample available to 'front-line professionals' is in line with recommendations for policy and practice from the most recent and comprehensive report on research on divorce and separation, and the implications for children in the UK, commissioned by the Rowntree foundation (Rodgers and Pryor, 1998, p. 7). They suggest that 'A number of policy and practice implications can be drawn, with caution, from the existing research findings:

- Some children and parents need professional support at the time of separation. Help for parents in dealing with their distress will assist them in supporting their children through the transition from one household structure to another. The availability of support services should be made known to parents going through separation.
- Support cannot be provided by specialist services alone. Parents are most likely to seek advice from GPs, teachers and family lawyers, who are often ill-equipped to help. Information and training for these groups may enable them to deal with families who do not require or wish for specialist help.
- Information for parents can also be helpful. It is important to allay the worries of many parents that separation itself can have a damaging and permanent effect on their children. It is equally important to convey the message that present and future factors, such as family conflict, could have detrimental effects. Parents should be encouraged to minimise the involvement of children in their disputes.
- There are likely to be benefits from enabling children to maintain contact with both their parents. Aside from circumstances where it is necessary to protect children from family violence or abuse, support services should facilitate the continuing involvement of non-custodial parents in their children's lives.
- Acknowledgement of diverse family forms by policy-makers and support groups is vital if families are to be helped to function in ways that are best for the health and well-being of their individual members. *Support may be just as important at times of repartnering as it is following separation*' [emphasis added].

As the findings suggest, families need support at the time of divorce and its aftermath, both from generic and specialist services. This book is intended for a wide range of professionals:

- Those in the 'front line' whose responsibilities and relationship with children and their families make them the first port of call when difficulties arise by virtue of their involvement at various points in the family's developmental life-cycle: These include general practitioners, teachers, health visitors, school nurses, social workers and school counsellors, for example.
- Those professionals who, from their own specialist perspectives, come into contact with the families at the time of separation and divorce. Counsellors, psychotherapists, family therapists, mediators, lawyers, court welfare officers, psychologists and psychiatrists, and others working in the areas of health, education, social services and the voluntary sector.

We hope that the way we have presented our ideas and illustrated them with examples from our experience with a clinical population can be useful to professionals in all these different settings.

Chapter 1 provides a research overview with some implications for direct work with children and parents at various points in the process of separation and divorce. Chapter 2 presents a theoretical framework for thinking about transitions drawing on ideas from attachment theory, family systems theory and the family life-cycle, and examines the divorce experience for children in the context of a developmental model of transitions. Chapters 3, 4 and 5 address separation and divorce from the parents' and children's perspectives respectively. In describing the model we have developed, in which we combine individual, couple and family work, these chapters pay particular attention to the different experiences of parents and children. Chapter 4 addresses the conflicts of interest between family members and the way in which a particular 'voice' may become dominant, with other voices in the family remaining submerged or silent. In Chapter 5 we focus on our work with children which places emphasis on helping children as well as parents to evolve a coherent story about their experiences, and we describe particular strategies we have evolved for working therapeutically with divorcing and post-divorce families.

Chapter 6 addresses issues of more extreme behaviour including violence and mental health problems in parents, and their implications both for children and for professionals. Chapter 7 looks at the impact of family reorganisation: the complexities of new relationships, stepparents, step and half-siblings, and the ways in which reordered families interrelate with the families that have preceded them and continue to coexist in different forms alongside them. In Chapters 8 and 9 we move to the 'front-line' context: schools and general practice (the 'family doctor') are the two settings to which all families have access and which, as research shows, provide the first port of call for parents seeking advice at the time of separation and divorce (Rodgers and Pryor, 1998).

The impact of family disruption on life at school for the children is often underestimated. Increasingly teachers have the responsibility to contain the anxieties and feelings experienced by children who find themselves in the middle of family turmoil. Sometimes the school is the only aspect of continuity in the child's otherwise changing life. Chapter 8 addresses appropriate ways for teachers to help pupils and their parents to cope with the aftermath of divorce, in the context of their role as educators. General practitioners, in their role as family doctors, have a relationship with families that often spans long periods of the family's life-cycle. Other professionals in primary care, such as health visitors and practice nurses, are also involved at various stages of family development. Whatever the circumstances, they represent a valuable resource for families facing divorce and its aftermath. In Chapter 9 we explore how to maximise the potential of the primary-care context for useful and meaningful contact with families at this stage.

Chapter 10 examines the specific issues affecting different professionals from different backgrounds who may come into contact with families at different stages of the divorce process. We consider issues for those working directly with children in the health, education and social services field, as well as the implications of divorce and separation for those working in the legal context and in the adult mental health field. Particular attention is paid to the skills involved in talking with children, and enabling children to talk in ways that feel safe and take account of the loyalty binds in which they find themselves.

Last but not least, we end with 'notes for parents', a summary of the things we think are important for parents to bear in mind for their children during times of separation and change.

The book draws on our experience of over 20 years of working with families, many of whom have gone through the process of separating, divorcing and remarrying. For some these processes have been more difficult and painful than others. We have become aware that children and parents need to evolve new narratives of their lives in order to move on, and from our work with families we have learned which factors can moderate the harmful effects of divorce and therefore contribute positively to family change (Gorell Barnes and Dowling, 1997; Dowling and Gorell Barnes, 1999).

We are grateful to the families we have worked with who have taught us so much about their dilemmas and suffering, but also about their resourcefulness, resilience and capacity for change. The examples throughout the book have been carefully disguised in respect to families' identities and circumstances in order to preserve confidentiality.

1

FAMILY CHANGE AND CHILDREN'S ANXIETIES

Family forms are changing, and diversity in family life is increasing. The idea of marriage as a permanent institution which allows children to look forward to spending their childhood within the same household has also changed; divorce becoming a reality in the lives of one in 20 children before they are four years old and one in four children under 16. Divorce has also therefore become an anxiety within the minds of many children whose parents are together, the wider experience of family life learnt through school and among friends creating ideas about the realities divorce entails and provoking anxieties about what might happen to their own family lives. In this book we hope to address some of the realities experienced by children as the family move through changes and transitions following the parental decision to divorce, anxieties about what will happen to them, to their brothers or sisters, to their mothers or fathers or pets in both the short term and the long term; anxieties about home, possible changes of school and sports teams and of friends, the changing fabric of everyday life.

The publication of the Exeter Study (Cockett and Tripp 1994), the study of a non-clinical population of children and parents in the west of England, emphasised a need families feel for services that address family break-up and family reordering to be available to parents and children once the decision to divorce has been taken. In that study parents emphasised how parenting ability is undermined at a time when parents most need to be strong. Parents are required to make important decisions regarding their own and their children's future, when they themselves are in emotional turmoil and surrounded by uncertainties. Among the things parents stated they would like was help in explaining divorce and separation to their children, and help in achieving better and more reliable contact with each other. Specialist services are unlikely to be funded on the scale required by the increases of family reordering. However, all professionals working in schools or in primary health care are likely to be in contact with parents and children going through divorce, and can become more confident about their ability to offer relevant support and information in relation to the dilemmas involved. In the chapters that follow we show how mothers and fathers try to address anxieties and conflict with each other and with their children, and some of the reasons why they find it difficult to do so. In that we are all involved in developing current knowledge about what is helpful to parents and children, who usually have very different positions in relation to divorce, we are sharing what we have learnt, translating the relevance of this knowledge into how it may be useful in other settings and raising further questions for the future.

The field of divorce research is now very large. The number of families on which the research described in this book is based is small, 50 children in all, belonging to 30 families, but our clinical work over 20 years is the backdrop to this focused study in which we have spent several hours with each family and very many hours with some. All this work was transcribed, enabling us to think about it in detail over time. We hope therefore to illuminate some of the subtle processes that help children and adults towards more positive outcomes.

We give particular emphasis to the different ways in which mothers and fathers respond to divorce, to children's post-divorce relationships with their resident and non-resident parents, and to the processes of adjustment involved for each member of the family. In presenting different patterns of coping with the divorce experience we will be focusing on a variety of parental styles, mainly acrimonious, sometimes apparently harmonious but concealing acute psychological distress. As well as looking in detail at some of the negative effects of acrimony, hostility, anger and violence on children, we will also describe how some of the different ways in which parents' attempts to manage changes 'as smoothly as possible', through not discussing processes that are going on around them, may not always be in the best interests of their children.

A focus on transitions: what makes them better and what makes them worse

In the process of working with divorcing and separating families we have moved from a focus on divorce itself, to a focus on transitions. Changes associated with divorce are connected to changes in the wider family system; and sometimes to changes in the larger structure of the children's world. Managing family life successfully after parental break-up is therefore connected to social systems outside the changing home, and the way these do or do not support family members at different points in the divorce process. The experiences accompanying divorce vary for each member of the family; for the husband/father, for the mother/wife and for each of the children. The ways in which each person copes or does not cope will be different. One family member managing well does not necessarily connect with other family members doing well, as processes of influence and mutual support change and reorganise. It seems likely from other research that where the parent who provides the primary residence is seen to be doing well by the children, this provides an ongoing sense of family life which in itself offers an important basis for the child's continuing sense of security, in spite of the separation. To see a parent continuing to regulate a familiar daily life not only provides an internal sense for the child that everything has not ended, but can also provide a model of everyday management skills that children themselves are likely to take on board (Ochiltree, 1990; Gorell Barnes et al., 1998). Concern about the emotional and physical well-being of the parent who no longer lives in the home, and worry about the part they will continue to play in the child's life is also of importance to the well-being of the child (Gorell Barnes et al., 1998).

In the early 1990s about 160 000 families with children under 16 went through an experience of parental divorce. Of these children, one in three was under five years old. A further 7000 children were between five and ten years old (Haskey, 1993). However, these figures do not convey the full picture of the transitions that occur among the population of young children in the UK. Until the last census the General Household Survey did not take account of cohabitation as a family form so that mothers and children who lived in these families which may have subsequently dissolved do not form part of the overall separation and divorce statistics (Roberts, 1995; Rogers and Pryor, 1998). The proportion of live births outside marriage has risen to just below one-third of all live births (30 per cent), so that many more young children may be expected to experience a parental separation without themselves appearing in the statistics relating to children and 'reordering' following marriage and divorce. Twenty per cent of these live births outside marriage have a father's name on the birth certificate, so that this unresearched population contains a proportion of 'living together while living apart' relationships which will affect those children who have formed a relationship with both parents in early childhood when such a relationship comes to an end (Kiernan and Estaugh, 1993). One small study in this area (Rose, 1992) showed how 10 out of 17 children of elective single mothers described themselves as having a 'ghost' father of whom they knew very little, but did not feel they could ask their mothers about. Mothers in turn did not like discussing the father with the children (a finding corroborated by Wren, 1997). Children accounted for a father's absence by blaming themselves for it and feeling rejected.

A majority of young children whose mothers have separated from their fathers are likely to experience further family relationship changes in the context of one or both parents repartnering. In the light of research evidence, any initial separation may therefore usefully be considered as part of a more complex series of potential transitions in the child's subsequent life. In thinking about families post-divorce, the term 'reordered' families has recently been used to take these wider changes into account, as well as to acknowledge the variety of separations experienced through changes in sexual relationship patterns outside marriage itself (Cockett and Tripp, 1994).

Short and long-term effects

Research from many countries has shown how aspects of the divorce experience have short-term negative effects for many children. The most marked disruptions in the individual functioning of family members, both for adults and children, are usually found in the first two years following divorce. Most studies report the establishment of new roles and relationships over a two-year period (Ahrons and Miller, 1993; Hetherington, 1989a; Isaacs, Leon and Donahue, 1987; Isaacs, 1988; Ochiltree, 1990). Children exposed to high-intensity parental conflict experience a wide range of emotional and behavioural difficulties (Amato and Rezac, 1994; Camara and Resnick, 1988; Elliott and Richards, 1992; Emery and Forehand, 1994; Jenkins, Smith and Graham, 1988; Jenkins and Smith, 1990).

It is important to recognise that although severe psychological and behavioural problems are two to three times more prevalent in children from divorced families than from non-divorced families, the meaning of these differences changes when we consider that many of them were present while their parents were still involved (Block and Gjerde, 1986). Seventy to eighty per cent of children do not show enduring problems following parental divorce, and Hetherington' s research has been particularly clear in emphasising this (Hetherington, 1992). There is now widely researched evidence showing the variety of children's and parents' responses to divorce and to the wide variation in lived experience that the idea of 'divorce' contains (Hetherington, 1989ab; Dunn et al., 1998; Gorell Barnes et al., 1998).

The long-term effects are much more complex to chart, since so many factors other than the divorce itself are likely to affect children's lives. The evidence on whether children from divorcing families are statistically more at risk in the long term for emotional disturbance than children whose parents have not divorced is conflicting. Some authors suggest that children's lives continue to be overshadowed by concern about the divorce in ways that are detrimental to their development (Wallerstein and Kelly, 1980), while others take the position that how children adapt will largely depend on how their parents manage the process (Emery and Forehand, 1994). Meta-analysis of 92 studies of divorce involving over 13 000 children has suggested very small differences between children from married and divorced families (Amato and Keith, 1991). However, children's ability to cope with the many challenges posed by divorce does not mean that they will not also have unhappy thoughts and feelings about it. Throughout this book we therefore try to indicate what in our experience promotes resilience in children. We use as our definition of resilience 'the maintenance of competent functioning despite an interfering emotionality' (Garmezy, 1991, p. 466). While there is little hard evidence about what helps children manage transitions or changes in family structures and family relationships better, we do have broad indications from a number of different sources. We know that where children maintain conflict-free relationships with both parents things go better, and that conflict-free relationships between parents correlates with higher self-esteem in children. The psychological well-being of the caretaking parent is important, as are the family dynamics in the larger extended family and the kind of supports that can be offered by them to parents and children in times of family change. We also know from different studies in the UK as well as elsewhere in the western hemisphere how difficult transitions can be, and we have a number of ideas about what makes the experience worse or intolerable for children. Continuing conflict between parents after divorce may be damaging, together with the aggravations brought about by too many other changes in their lives which may amplify a sense of loss and powerlessness .

While divorce itself contains many different changes for children in relation to the break-up of the former family household and the loss of the daily presence of one parent in their lives, it is also for many children a time when a parent re-partners and a new family arrangement is formed which includes an adult that they do not know. For many children divorce is accompanied or swiftly followed by a parent starting to live with someone else. This is likely to bring about an expectation that a child will make a new attachment to a new adult at a time when they have not yet become familiar or adapted to the changes in their now-separated original family. We have no idea how many cohabitations, partnerships or intimate 'friendship' arrangements between a parent and a new lover or partner, in which a child has begun to form relationships with the new adult, subsequently break up. Such break-ups may create further losses in children's lives. It is also to be noted that many children do not allow themselves to get close to the new 'friends' of their parents, both out of wariness and out of loyalty to their 'other' parent. In the experience of the divorce project, a larger proportion of children became involved with a subsequent adult relationship between one or both parents and a new partner within two years. A few of these relationships subsequently broke up with bitterness, sometimes to the children's relief but occasionally to their sorrow (see Chapter 7).

In briefly outlining the fluidity of the current scene of marriage, lone parenthood, cohabitation, relationship breakdown and repartnering, we are drawing attention to the large and varied nature of the attachment relationships which many of the children known to professionals in all primary health care and educational settings will experience. What may the effects of these frequently changing relationships be on a child's ability to negotiate his or her own course through development in good-enough ways? Where may parents lose sight of important connecting threads for children as their own relationships change, and where may the danger points in transitions lie? 'Danger points' may be factors that contribute to increased vulnerability or threaten a precariously maintained sense of self put together in the context of a number of changing relationship patterns. When any two people form a second or subsequent relationship it is not simply the couple and their children who are involved. Children may also find a range of relationships that are built in alongside the new adult partner such as step 'siblings', bringing with them larger issues of the joining of different family cultures. Conversely, what are the protective factors, aspects of the relationship between parent and child, between children and their siblings, between children and the wider family, or children and their peers or their daily world outside the home, that contribute to a resilient sense of self in spite of life transitions? How can professionals both be sensitive to stress points as well as able to offer children a different positive experience of themselves by doing the job they see themselves professionally equipped to do on the child's behalf, whether it is maintaining the child's health as the family doctor, or developing their minds and bodies in the context of school?

Family break-up: is it a useful concept?

We are aware that in talking of 'family break-up' there is always a danger of pathologising life transitions that many people also experience as intrinsically freeing. Parental separation does not always mean family break-up although it does mean family change. Men and women may develop new aspects of themselves when freed from relationships that they have found constraining, disqualifying or abusive. While the relationship between sexual partners ceases, and the living arrangement in which this relationship was housed changes, adults and children also develop new resources and solutions to the potential disconnections created by divorce, in particular new ways of maintaining satisfying patterns of relationship. Focusing on these new resources, and the sense of developing well-being that often accompanies them, is likely to be an important contribution professionals can make to parents struggling to develop new ways of managing their children's changing lives and relationships.

Anger and bitterness

Studies from different parts of the UK have highlighted the anger, conflict and bitterness that often accompanies divorce. Walker and colleagues, in their study of 400 divorcing families in Newcastle, have in particular cautioned against the danger of an implicit 'ideal-type' post-divorce family which may organise professionals' beliefs and place too great an emphasis on a cooperative future. One of the dangers of a middle-class movement, influenced by ideas of 'seamless' divorce and mediation, is that it can place too much expectation on 'agreement' between ex-partners. For at least a quarter of families in the recent study in Newcastle this was out of the question (Simpson, Mcarthy and Walker, 1995). The Exeter Study also showed that of 152 children whose families were reordered, fewer than half had contact with the non-resident parent two years later. We must take note of the direct evidence from these and other studies that for children, divorce is rarely easy and that professionals need to understand the processes involved in detail rather than dismissing the disruption of relationships as normative events from which children will recover in time. Disruptive processes are likely to include difficulties in communication between parents who are no longer living together, as well as patterns of quarrelling and aggressive behaviour. Loss of self-esteem as individuals struggle to establish their own beliefs about how to reconstruct their lives and their social networks, while negotiating what is important for their children, is common in separating couples.

In our work, models of theory that frame stressful life experience in pathologising ways has long been replaced by the wish to consider and learn more about the intricate daily factors that render children or parents more vulnerable, side by side with those that may protect them against risk, the development of what is known as resilience. One of us (ED) has in particular represented a developmental perspective in taking the differences in children's responses into account. Younger children in this study, for example, have shown themselves less able to understand the realities of what has led to a divorce or to understand what divorce entails, and may be more likely to think it is their own fault. Older children are more likely to have a range of classmates or peers with similar life experiences with whom to make comparisons, although this does not necessarily relieve them of a sense of personal responsibility.

Both authors have been interested in thinking about transitions following divorce within a 'systemic framework'. This framework involves considering how the characteristics of individual family members and the interactions between them play a part in how each person may feel and behave at any time as the family changes shape. Fluctuations between the different 'subsystems' – father/children, mother/children, father/mother, sister/brother – affect individual and family well-being, particularly changes in the former marital partnership, ex-husband and ex-wife. Other subsystem changes include the entrances of new 'partners', which may affect the arrangements for parent–child contact time, as well as creating conflicts of loyalty in children.

Mothers, fathers and children in the immediate post-separation period

The majority of children, following divorce, live with their mothers, although the small proportion who had primary residence with their fathers mirrored the national average in the UK (estimated at between 11 and 14 per cent). One of our goals was to involve both parents with the work done in the divorce project, and to challenge the 'national average' of fathers who drop out by the end of the second year following divorce (estimated in different studies at between 30 and 40 per cent; Bradshaw and Millar, 1991; Simpson, McCarthy and Walker, 1995).

According to other research, the quality of relationships between mothers and their children seems to vary in relation to the gender of the child. Single mothers and daughters can develop close harmonious relations, whereas single mothers and sons often experience greater childrearing stress involving angry exchanges over issues of maternal control (Hetherington, 1993). However, a number of the boys we saw presented with very close relationships to their mothers, whereas a number of the girls' relationships with their mothers encompassed angry and critical exchanges. Mothers were more likely to express concern about closeness with sons than with daughters, since they felt it might be inhibiting their sons' relationships with friends or be related to learning difficulties that were also reported at the time. This concern over boys who are close may reflect wider gender issues about what is seen as appropriate behaviour for boys; just as fear of negativity in a relationship with a daughter is framed by a wider social belief that girls and their mothers should be close.

Some of the effects of living in a one-parent-headed household reported in research highlight some differences between children in clinical and non-clinical samples. Children in non-clinical samples have been described as more autonomous, as having less adult supervision, as spending less time in the company of adults. They are described as developing greater competence in relation to household tasks and as taking pride in participating in the smooth functioning of the family. Such generalisations are clearly age-related and are also connected to the length of time a family has itself reorganised in relation to a lone-parent-headed structure. Our sample of parents, alongside other clinically-based samples such as those of Wallerstein and her colleagues (Wallerstein and Kelly, 1980), did not necessarily frame such features of family behaviours as autonomy in positive ways. For example children's greater autonomy and participation in decision-making often posed further dilemmas for adults who felt their authority weakened by the loss of power the changes following divorce had entailed (fathers and mothers, residential as well as non-residential parents). They might experience the diminishing of distinctions between the generations as leaving them more 'controlled' by their children and less free to be 'in charge'. We note that parents in the Exeter study, a non-clinical UK sample, also reported that their authority was weakened by their own sense of vulnerability. Attention towards helping parents to strengthen their decision-making abilities in appropriate ways is therefore likely to be important for professionals to focus on.

We all need to be aware that images of 'motherhood' are in constant social negotiation and reconstruction through the images created by government policy-making and the kind of debates this generates, as well as by journalism, the media and by mothers themselves. Social construction is concerned with the ways in which our identities are multiple and complex, related to the society and the changing times in which images are produced. To be a mother of children following divorce in the first years of the new millennium will be a different experience in many ways from being a mother of children following divorce in the 1960s; just as to live in London with children will be different from living in Cyprus, Barbados, Rio or Delhi. Nonetheless, there will be features of the role of mothers post-divorce which are likely to have some constancy, independent of time and place. In carrying out the role of mother a woman may still find herself unfavourably compared on many counts with women still married in two-parent families. Mothers more than fathers continue to be seen as having the responsibility for their children 'turning out right'. While the debate on what kind of family is most likely to help children 'turn out right' has undergone radical shifts in the last decade, certain kinds of family have continued to be privileged above others in many public debates, often in the face of evidence that contradicts the moral high ground that is being defended. Lone-parent families have consistently been attacked for failing to be 'real families' and continue to be described as though they are a unitary family form, rather than a label that conceals many different functional structures for bringing up children (Burghes, 1995). Recent research has challenged many of the stereotypes about lone parents, showing that children raised in fatherless families from infancy may experience greater warmth and interaction with their mother, and be more securely attached to her (Tasker and Golumbok, 1997).

Fathers

How do men understand, think, feel and express the differences of fatherhood in the context of parenting post-divorce? How is this contextualised by their economic resources, family histories and larger cultural beliefs? Motherhood and fatherhood are themselves constructed in many different ways which are then in turn challenged by divorce (Burghes, Clarke and Cronin, 1997). For example, dominant notions of femininity (femaleness) which are involved in the traditional beliefs about motherhood held within differing cultures are complemented within those cultures by beliefs about masculinity and the appropriate balance between the genders. The notion of men being dominant or strong (often traditionally linked with violence towards women and children) requires modifying, and other aspects of self have to be developed and elaborated for post-divorce parenting to become viable for men. In our work with parents we have taken the position that there is no fixed relationship between a parent's gender and what they are able to do or not to do on behalf of their children. We would like to suggest that there is as much danger in making general assumptions about lone fathers and their inability to parent as there is about lone mothers, having found a great variety in the range and ability of men to parent within our own small sample of families going through post-divorce processes.

Other work carried out in the context of looking at changing family roles and norms (Gorell Barnes et al., 1997) had led one of us (GGB) to a particular interest in the comparative neglect of fathers in the allocation of post-divorce responsibilities. Two small projects carried out in the context of the divorce project further expanded this interest. One studied further the way in which men's own perception of what constitutes acceptable behaviour for men and for women as parents related to their ability to take on commitment to parenting following divorce. In this study, Hart (1994) showed that many factors influenced the development of post-divorce fathering roles. Men's own ability to develop flexibility in arrangements for looking after children was found to relate to their capacity to take on patterns of parenting which include doing jobs formerly defined as belonging to women, or more usually seen culturally within the domain of 'mothering'. Adams

(1996) has in addition found that the experience of having had a good father oneself, as well as ongoing support from other men doing a similar job, makes an important difference to men's ability to continue fathering on their own, a job that many describe as at times a frustrating and painful experience.

The second study (Bratley, 1995) looked at men's experiences and difficulties in attempting to maintain contact with their children where the court had ordered that this should be under supervision. The study took place in a London contact centre. A developing concern emerging from this project, as well as from our own clinical work, revolved around how to offer psychological as well as educational support to fathers to help them develop parenting skills that were appropriate to their children's ages. Kraemer (1995) has argued that women still provide the context in which men learn parenting skills; and while researchers have neither proved nor disproved this theory, it is likely to be one aspect of the high drop-out in fathers' contact with their children in the two years following divorce. What some fathers do is almost invariably shared with, or dependent on, the cues of his partner, so that his experience of fatherhood behaviour is seen by him as essentially intertwined with his coupledom. Following this logic, when the coupledom is severed a father may be unsure how to behave and the move to a personal parenting identity will be laborious and painful. This is especially likely to be so when separation has been acrimonious and hostile, and a father has nowhere he can take a child to what he sees as a 'home'.

In our experience, fathers differed greatly in the length of time they took to feel competent and confident as parents in the absence of their former wives. In part this related to the degree to which a mother 'allowed' a father to develop his own style of post-divorce parenting independent of watchful dictates about 'correct' behaviour. For some fathers who were not able to develop appropriate skills, to be viewed critically by a former wife created severe stress. In these situations a developmental and educative approach which allowed a father to place his own thinking within a wider framework was welcomed. However, some fathers had been very committed to parenting throughout their children's lives, and in some instances had been equal caregivers to children alongside mothers who were working full-time. In these situations arguments around 'what is best for the child' often had a competitive edge of 'whose expertise is going to be valued more highly' in which the child could become a loser either way.

If there is growing evidence that fathers can be competent, loving and committed parents, how will the debate about whether it is better to maintain contact with both parents if they quarrel, or better for the child to lose contact with one so as not to be affected by the continual conflict, move forward in the next decade? Answers about the relationship conditions which may influence a decision either way are likely to be refined through further research studies. Currently we know that when divorcing couples voluntarily seek or accept joint parental responsibility and are able to coparent without excessive conflict, fathers are more likely to stay involved in a positive way (Maccoby and Mnookin, 1992), and that this in turn will be of benefit to their children. A warm relationship with an authoritative non-resident father has been found to be associated with higher self-esteem, better social and cognitive competencies and fewer behavioural problems in children (Hetherington and Stanley-Hagan, 1995). Furstenberg and his colleagues looking at teenagers' perceptions of their relationships with their non-resident fathers found that 76 per cent reported that their fathers were interested in them and loved them even when contact was infrequent. It seems likely that children can identify with and by extension establish a positive relationship with their non-resident father even when they see them very little but on a regular basis (Furstenberg, Morgan and Allison, 1987).

What are the advantages of shared parenting for the children

Maccoby and her colleagues (1990, 1993), as well as other researchers using different names for similar classifications of behaviour, have identified three patterns of parenting:

1. *Cooperative,*... in which parents talk with each other on matters that relate to the children, avoid arguments and support rather than undermine each other's parenting.

2. *Conflicted,...* in which parents talk with each other about their children but with criticism, acrimony defensiveness and attempts to undermine each other's parenting.
3. *Disengaged,...* in which both are involved with their children but adopt what Furstenberg has described as a parallel parenting model. Each parent adopts their own style but does not interfere with each other's parenting. Communication with each other is avoided except through the children, which reduces the likelihood of direct conflict but centralises the child.

As noted earlier, and discussed at length in Chapter 6, feelings of anger and resentment may be very hard for many divorced parents to control, and even two years after a divorce about one-quarter of parents are still involved in conflicted parenting (Maccoby and Mnookin, 1992; Simpson, McCarthy and Walker, 1995). Children suffer from the adverse effects of exposure to parental conflict and often feel caught in the middle (Cockett and Tripp, 1994; Hetherington, 1993). Children in the middle may act as 'go-betweens' and may learn to exploit their parents and to play one off against the other. For many divorcing couples the conflict may escalate rather than diminish after the divorce. Simpson *et al.* (1995) have shown how negative relationships may become worse following divorce, or sharply deteriorate from a neutral to an acrimonious style of discourse. In these circumstances fathers may reduce contact with their children in order to avoid further argument. The practicality of joint residence in the context of continued conflict is problematic. The work involved in helping parents to develop problem-solving and dispute-resolution skills, and ways of coming to agreement without escalating anger and tension, is considerable and time-consuming, although in our view possible. However, time taken by professionals to help parents develop and maintain positive parenting is currently not legislated for, and remains outside mediation structures within the terms that services are currently set up.

Recent work has suggested that non-resident fathers who are unable to have as much contact with their children as they would like are particularly at risk of developing psychological illness (Kitson and Holmes, 1992). The ambiguity and sense of powerlessness reported by many fathers following the loss of daily contact with their children has been reported in other studies on both sides of the Atlantic (Kruk, 1992; Simpson, McCarthy and Walker, 1995).

Fathers and mothers with joint residence

Joint residence honours the wishes of parents to offer their children equality in parenting. In the long term, the effects of joint residence are positive where neutrality, or at best goodwill, is maintained between parents: fathers become more comfortable with parenting and more involved in the emotional and practical aspects of childcare. Mothers, similarly, find themselves less burdened by childcare responsibilities and more able to pursue other interests (Bender, 1994; Kelly, 1993). However, from the child's point of view research shows different things and the superiority of joint residence over a child caring primary residence with one or other parent has not been established. (Hetherington and Stanley-Hagan, 1997) The detailed weekly hassles joint parenting involves can create tension in children, specially if conducted in front of them or through them, using the child as message bearer.

Other variations of joint care considered in research include alternations of child care between parents on a weekly or split-week basis, or between school weeks and weekends. These were all reflected in our sample. In one family seen before the study officially started, the children remained in one household and the parents moved in and out. The paramount advantage of any of these 'equal' arrangements, usually agreed to rather than proposed by the mothers we have talked with, is that neither parent feels relegated to the position of visitor. Each parent has some time off from child care responsibilities, and indeed several mothers have subsequently confessed to enjoying their regular 'weekends off' as an opportunity to reclaim and develop their own lives. However, since all the parents we saw came because there was initial or ongoing disagreement between them, it is also important to note the awkwardness experienced by parents and by their children who sometimes felt either dispossessed of a clear 'home' or of their own minds in the context of adapting on a frequent and regular basis to disputing parents' different world views.

Resilience and parental divorce

In ending this highly selective review of research related to some of the effects of divorce on children's well-being, we would like to emphasise the need to consider stress and coping processes as interacting at a number of different levels. These include social as well as psychological and emotional processes, each of which may contribute in different ways to resilience in children, in spite of the stresses they are living through. We therefore end the chapter with some highlights from different research studies, including our own, which show some of the family and social factors contributing to children's resilience.

- There are many *shapes* of family, and children have been shown to do well in families that are of different shapes, both before and after divorce. Divorce does not end family life, although it changes its shape.
- At a social level, the variety of family forms in the UK needs to be accepted and normalised through many sources such as the media and journalism as well as within school education programmes. Parents themselves need confidence in their own form of family life if children are not to feel disadvantaged.
- Where parents maintain conflict-free relationships with each other, and where children maintain conflict-free relationships with their parents, things go better. All professionals should become aware of the negative effects of conflict on children and consider how they can help parents from their own professional position to reduce this.
- Children need story lines about a parent who does not form an ongoing part of their lives. In lone-parent families where a mother still carries anger about a non-participant father this may be more difficult than in families where a planned lone parenthood has been chosen. Whereas lesbian households and families formed by donor sperm or egg are getting together to create children's stories and literature that gives children permission to think about their origins, there is some evidence that lone parents may be reluctant to do this and that children remain confused about the role of men in their families.

- A good relationship with one parent can make an important difference to a child at times when a marital relationship is bad, or when one parent has a bad relationship with the child.
- Good relationships between brothers and sisters (siblings) will also make a difference.
- Parents and children may need support from their wider families at times of family change. They do not need criticism.
- Social support from adults outside the family and from children's friends, is related to children's positive adjustment following divorce.
- School experiences are likely to be of great importance. Attention and warmth shown by teachers are key factors.

While the above factors all relate to children's resilience, and research shows that most children cope with the many challenges of divorce, they are also likely to have unhappy thoughts and feelings about both the divorce and their parents' experience in the life that follows. We address some of these experiences in the following chapters.

Theoretical Framework: Transitions and Risk Factors in Separation and Divorce

2

The aim of this chapter is to explore how children develop through the various stages of the family life-cycle, and how these processes are affected by the experience of a parental divorce. Our ideas are based on the premise that growth and development only acquire meaning in a given context. If children grow up in an environment where not only their basic physical needs but also their emotional needs are met, they will develop secure attachments to their care-givers and gradually evolve a narrative about themselves as loveable and likeable which will form the basis of further positive relationships. We are concerned with examining the impact that separation and divorce has on children at different developmental stages.

Attachment theory provides a useful model for understanding children's development in the context of relationships, and Bowlby's ideas (1988) have had a crucial impact in terms of understanding the effect of early relationships on relationships later in life. In particular, attachment theory postulates that the relationship a child develops with his mother or caregiver is crucial to the development of future relationships, and research confirms that the more secure the early relationship with the caregiver is, the more the infant is able to explore the world around in the knowledge that there is a 'secure base' to return to.

Main (see for example Main, Kaplan and Cassidy, 1985) has used the notion of *internal working models* to explain how young children represent and construct the experience of a relationship.

The internal working model of the young child's relationship with a parent will be formed out of a history of the parent–child interaction, including the child's efforts to regain the parent even when the parent is absent. The *working model of the relationship* will not reflect an *objective picture of the parent*, but rather the *history of the perceived responses to the child* (Dowling, 1993). Therefore, a child whose parents are perceived as available and helpful is likely to construct a model of self as coping but also worthy of help. Children who experience their parents as lacking in response or unavailable, will tend to build a representation of themselves as unlovable and unworthy (Bowlby, 1977).

Attachment behaviours represent a web of complex interactions which develop between mother and baby in a mutual, interlocking pattern from the time the baby is born and which continue over the early weeks and months. As the child develops, new attachment relationships develop with father, siblings and other reliable caregivers. The proximity-seeking behaviours towards the attachment figures increase with mobility (6–7 months), but also the child begins to show signs of selective attachments by protesting at separation and showing fear of strangers.(8–12 months). Nearly all attachment behaviours are, in fact, heightened in stressful or fearful situations. We also know from research that the parent–child attachment is influenced by the conditions of proximity. In recognition of this, current practice in hospitals encourages contact between mothers and babies from birth. Although research has been mainly focused on mothers, some research suggests that fathers' attachment behaviours, at least initially, are virtually identical to those of the mothers, but that over the first few months fathers develop distinctive roles (Parke and Tinsley, 1981).

Lamb and his colleagues (Lamb *et al.*, 1982) studied a group of caregiving fathers in Sweden and concluded that regardless of the caregiving role, mothers still talked and held the babies more. This study suggests that gender could have a more important influence on parental behaviour than the caregiving role. Lamb (1997) provides a comprehensive summary of current knowledge on fathers and fatherhood, father–child relationships and the influence of fathers in the development of the child.

Research in the adult attachment field suggests that the ability to put together a coherent story about one's life is connected to the capacity to make secure attachments in future life (Main, Kaplan and Cassidy, 1985).

If parents are to provide children with a secure base from which they can develop emotionally and socially they need:

- An understanding of children's wishes for proximity, attention and responsiveness, not as naughty, demanding or unreasonable, but as a developmental expression of their needs. The more this need is rejected or unmet the more the demand will increase and eventually it will be expressed in the form of physical or psychological symptoms.
- A recognition that the commonest source of children's anger is the frustration of their desire for love and care, and their anxiety usually reflects the uncertainty as to whether parents will continue to be available.

The pre-school years

As children grow and develop, the balance between exploratory behaviour and the familiar secure base of the family gradually changes. Children's experience of the wider world of the playgroup or nursery school will be greatly influenced by the frame given by the parents to this transition. Preparing the child for the transition, explaining what is to be expected, visiting so that the child has a concrete picture of what to expect are all ways in which parents can help children adapt to the new situation. However, the emphasis on the excitement of the transition has to be combined with an awareness of the impact that the separation from the caregiver will have on the child. At this stage of development children need concrete explanations, for example of the time that they will be away, the time they will be collected, and what will be different from home – friends, size of the place, food, and so on.

The divorce experience and the pre-school years

When children are at the pre-school stage, parents are often overwhelmed by the demands, both physical and emotional, made on them by their children. This constant state of responding to immediate demands often results in a strain in the parents' relationship, as the more basic needs of each individual have to be postponed or even go unattended in the service of the parenting task. Parents need and should have considerable support at this stage of their family life. Extended family and friends are the most obvious sources, but the neighbourhood and the community in which families live may provide a range of supportive contexts which vary from the more informal gatherings of parents with young children to more formal settings such as toddlers groups, family centres, and so on. Parents bringing up young children in isolation are more vulnerable to the inherent pressures of bringing up a family as they lack the supportive structures provided by a wider network of relationships.

When parents decide to separate, the decision may follow a period of dissatisfaction and frustration. The relationship may have been deteriorating in a more dramatic way, rows may have become increasingly violent, either verbally or physically, or it may be that the couple have simply 'grown apart' and, for whatever reason, the decision to separate seems the only option available. That decision may be seen by one or both partners as the best solution to their particular dilemma in their particular circumstances. Intense feelings of anger, loss, pain and distress may dominate the day-to-day interactions, and communication between the partners may become increasingly fraught. It can then become difficult to consider the needs of the children particularly as they conflict with the decision that the couple have made.

In the midst of the emotional turmoil, triggered off by leaving or being left, there are likely to be financial pressures and possible forthcoming changes such as moving house and leaving friends and support systems. Parents have to bear in mind what children need at that particular time to cope with the transition.

How, when and what to tell the children

What kind of explanation do young children need and what can they take in? Is it better to say nothing, to lie, to say daddy is working away, to pretend that nothing has happened? All these and many more questions exercise parents at a time when they are themselves confused and overwhelmed by a mixture of emotions. Most parents worry first and foremost about what is best for their children.

Children need an explanation which is understandable and appropriate to their stage of development. Even at a very early age the child can be helped by a parent putting into words what is happening around them. This is particularly important if the change is going to involve not seeing their parents as frequently or having to visit them elsewhere. In certain circumstances it may involve explaining the fact that the parent has disappeared from their lives altogether. It can be difficult for parents to separate the explanation given to the children from their own feelings of hurt, disappointment and loss. From the point of view of the children it is essential that the distinction is made clear between the couple being unable to live together, and the parent–child relationship continuing. This is very difficult for the children to understand but they will be helped if the parents articulate this distinction for them.

The following is an example of what might be said to a three-year-old:

Parent: Mummy and daddy are not going to live together any more. Daddy is going to live in…
Child: Why?
Parent: Mummy and daddy argue a lot and they will get on better if they don't live in the same place. But we both love you very much and you will see daddy every week/weekend etc. Daddy will come and get you on Wednesday afternoon after swimming. Wednesday is swimming day and it is going to be daddy's day as well.

From a very early age children feel bound by loyalty to their parents. They often think that expressing their feelings or even asking a question about one parent may upset the other. Children become 'parent watchers', taking care not to upset their parents even at the expense of bearing the upset themselves. In terms of research evidence, Fergusson, Lynskey and Horwood, (1994) in New Zealand found that parental separation seemed to have less impact on children's cognitive development when it occurred before entry to school. In other words, separation appears to have more marked effects on school-age children than pre-school children. These findings confirm those of Amato and Keith (1993).

Effects of the marital break-up on the capacity to parent

The end of the relationship, however acrimonious and difficult, is a complex process in which the sense of loss will coexist with a powerful sense of relief, particularly for those who have experienced violence. However, there is commonly also anxiety and guilt about the effect of the separation on the children. At a time when the parents are experiencing a disorganisation in their adult attachment, it becomes difficult to keep the parenting task first and foremost in their thinking. Parents may become depressed and distracted by their own thoughts, preoccupied with a new world of pressures both practical and emotional. These may interfere with the capacity to bear the children's needs in mind. Either parent may also be involved in a new relationship which has not been explained to the child.

As a result of the break up, children may have a strong need to be reassured of their parents' continuing love and care, but may be experienced by a parent as demanding or difficult. It is at a time when parents' emotional resources are most drained by the conflict and its consequences that the children most need emotional support.

Claire, aged four, was beginning to get used to her father seeing her regularly, after a period of inconsistent and erratic arrangements for contact with him. She had also met Rachel, father's new partner. During one of her contact visits, father told Claire, with great excitement, that she was going to have a step-brother or sister soon. 'Wouldn't it be lovely', he said, 'you will be the big sister and will help to change the baby's nappies'. Subsequent visits became very fraught, Claire was being very attention-seeking and clingy and was refusing to eat almost everything that father or Rachel offered. Father, feeling caught between his pregnant wife's feelings and his daughter's behaviour, took the easy way out. Weekends with him became less and less frequent for Claire. The nursery teacher began noticing changes in Claire's behaviour, and, wondering if these might be connected to her stepmother's pregnancy, talked to the mother about it. Claire was being aggressive towards younger children and had broken the doll's bath in the Wendy house. In discussion with father it became possible to recognise Claire's worries about losing her special relationship with him.

Parents can be helped to understand the developmental needs of their children and encouraged to respond appropriately. Extended family and friends can provide support and practical help. Teachers, health visitors and general practitioners can offer useful advice and suggestions. The role of these professionals will be examined in detail in Chapters 8, 9 and 10.

The school years

When a child starts school most families go through one of the most important transitions in their developmental life-cycle. The school world with its different setting, rules and ethos, presents a challenge for the child to connect the two worlds of home and school. School may be a completely new experience for the child and their parents in the case of the first born, or it may be quite familiar territory for a second born who would have been to the playground many times to collect their older brother or sister. Either way there will be a range of new experiences, involving separation from the parents as well as adjusting to the new environment. Although many children will have experienced previous transitions at a pre-school level, such as attending play group or nursery, the start of full-time education is an important developmental marker.

Teachers are 'in loco parentis' and from the start the relationship between the family and the school, however cooperative, will also include, perhaps less consciously, elements of competition as to who knows best or who can be a better parent. During the school years the child's academic progress and their social and emotional development will be affected by what is happening around them both at home and at school. Sometimes the tense atmosphere at home will result in difficulties in concentrating. Likewise, events at school will impact on the way a child behaves at home. Children find different ways of coping with stressful situations and one way is to keep the two worlds of home and school very separate. All parents will know of instances of bullying when parents were only told once things had got out of hand.

Divorce and the school

In the face of family turmoil the school can potentially be a place which can offer safety and continuity in the middle of a major disruption in children's lives, and school policies, organisation and the curriculum can help children and families affected by separation and divorce (Cox and Desforges, 1987). Research has shown that schools can help to counteract the vulnerability that children can display at times of conflict at home.

The Exeter study (Cockett and Tripp, 1994), one of the most significant studies of the impact of divorce on children in the UK, interviewed 152 children from two age groups (9–10 and 13–14) and their parents about their experiences of living in intact and reordered families. Half the children were living with both parents and half were in families 'reordered' by separation or divorce. The study showed that children in reordered families were more likely to report having received extra help with school work. The authors interpret this finding as evidence of supportive structures within the school rather than as indicating that children in reordered families were underachieving. School changes had occurred more frequently among children in reordered families. Ten per cent of children in reordered families compared with 5 per cent in intact families reported feelings of isolation as a result of problems with friends following a change of school. There were no significant differences between the two groups in terms of children reporting difficulties with teachers. However, parents in reordered families were significantly more likely to report truanting behaviour in their children.

Teachers reported less contact with parents in reordered families than with parents in intact families. The group with whom they had least contact was lone parents, who themselves reported difficulties in attending parents' evenings because of transport and child-care difficulties. The implication of divorce for children in the school context will be discussed more fully in Chapter 8.

The primary school years (5–11)

Infant school (5–7)

Entry into the school world represents an important life transition which marks the widening of the context in which children will function and the arena for their intellectual, emotional and social development. Decisions made by the parents about what school the child should go to will be based on beliefs about what is important for their child. Whether the school is local, religious and cultural factors, as well as size, reputation in the neighbourhood and ethos will influence such a decision and will have a bearing on the construction of the child's identity during their school years. Parents may have strongly held, and quite different, beliefs about what school is best, and the child of separated parents may be caught in a battle between the parents around schooling decisions.

Andrea, aged seven, was quite unhappy in her school and felt she had no friends. Her parents held very different views about Andrea's unhappiness. Mother, who herself had felt isolated at school, was more sympathetic and was prepared to consider a change. Andrea's father, on the other hand, was totally opposed to a change and found it very difficult to listen to Andrea's pleas. Andrea's unhappiness began to manifest itself in other areas. She was complaining of headaches and dizzy spells with no physical cause when she was referred to the clinic. In the course of our work it was possible to address Andrea's unhappiness and link it to her symptoms. The parents gradually felt able to move from their very entrenched positions to examine Andrea's worries and agreed to work together towards finding the best solution for Andrea. This involved consultation with the school but also exploring other options. Andrea felt relieved by her parents' new cooperative stance and began to trust that they were taking her plight seriously rather than just fighting each other. As she was freed from the responsibility for convincing each of them of her unhappiness, her dizzy spells became less frequent.

Much has been said about teaching methods and what is 'good' for children academically. However, despite the increasing proportion of children who truant, who get excluded from school earlier and earlier and the difficulties the schools experience with children who fail to respond to the social and academic demands placed upon them, little attention is paid to the emotional needs of children in the context of the classroom. As many teachers will be aware, it is important to recognise the effect that family disruption may have on children's learning.

At the age of five, children have an enormous interest in the world around them, and opportunities for discovery and learning are available in many ways. However, the capacity for the child to take in and process new stimuli, to understand and make sense of new experiences, will be determined by the sense of emotional well-being which will enhance his capacity to learn. Children who, in Bowlby's terms, feel 'loveable', that is who have experienced a safe environment in which they have met with approval, love and security, will be freer to explore new relationships in the school context. Teachers will be seen as benign adults, capable of nurture as well as setting limits which will make the new world safe. The social context will be enlarged and the playground will provide a laboratory for children to experiment with making new relationships, taking turns, winning and losing and all the various possibilities which will lead to establishing an identity as part of a peer group.

In contrast, a child whose world has been one of neglect, criticism and denigration will have great difficulty trusting adults and peers, and the new context will be approached with caution, anxiety or even aggression in order to preempt any attack on themselves. It will take a lot of time and effort, as many teachers will testify, to make an anxious and insecure child begin to trust others sufficiently to feel able to learn from them.

The two worlds of home and school are held together in the child's mind and the experiences children have of one will have an effect on their adjustment to the other. The child starting school will have to integrate different ways of doing things, different rules, and may for the first time be exposed to cultural differences which will be interesting and enriching but which also will demand tolerance, acknowledgement and acceptance of difference.

The impact of divorce in the primary school years

As children begin to explore the world of school and adapt to it, the security of the home base is all important. The realisation that the home as they know it, with two parents in it, is coming to an end can be a shattering experience for a child. Some will have been exposed to continuing conflict and arguments, some will have witnessed a cold 'silence and withdrawal' pattern of relationship between parents, and for some the tensions between the parents will have been contained and the exposure to conflict limited. Some children will have experienced verbal or physical violence, or witnessed it from one parent to the other during the period leading to the separation.

Perhaps not surprisingly, even young children jealously guard the privacy of what goes on in the family home, and first and foremost feel very loyal to their parents. Parents in turn may be too caught up in their own turmoil to think of informing the school about what is going on in the family. Many will feel strongly that 'it is none of their business'. The school will therefore be in the dark regarding the possible emotional pressures and distress children may be experiencing. However, there are many ways in which they may be made aware of the consequences. It is not uncommon for children to find it difficult to concentrate (as they will be preoccupied with what is going on at home) or to start 'playing up', perhaps in an attempt to test out whether their behaviour will make others leave. They may also exhibit aggressive behaviour towards other children, which could be indicative of anxiety about whether they can hold on to relationships, or it may be a repetition of what they have witnessed at home (see Chapter 6).

At home, children may revert to earlier patterns of behaviour in an attempt to deal with what appears to be an unsafe world. Clinging behaviour, nightmares and difficulties going to bed are some of the symptoms which can indicate the state of mind of a child at the time of a family break-up. There might also be reluctance to go to school, sometimes associated with the fear in the child's mind that the other parent might leave. These may be temporary indicators that a child is troubled by the loss of the family as they have known it, and provided they are dealt with in a sensitive and reassuring manner they will probably pass. However, it is often quite difficult for parents to reconcile their own feelings with accepting that the children are experiencing a profound sense of loss and need to be helped to express it in order to move on to the next stage in their lives.

Junior school (7–10)

Although this transition is often underestimated in terms of the children's experience, it is a significant marker of their development. Some primary schools have infant and junior departments housed in separate buildings, and even in the same building there is an understanding that the children are going to be expected to display a greater level of responsibility and autonomy, and the demands on them will now be greater in terms of their cognitive and emotional development. The Standard Attainment Tests (SATs) to be given to all seven-year-olds in state schools in England and Wales are an indicator of the attempt to test the expected levels of knowledge and skills for that age group and to compare children's development. The effect of the tests on children and their families has been notably understated. The increasing importance of school and peers is a feature of this developmental stage as the children branch out into relationships outside the family context.

The impact of divorce

For many children the pain and sadness of the break up of the family will inevitably involve changes in terms of moving house, maybe moving school and having to cope with a new context, making new friends and leaving what is familiar behind. At the time of such a major transition further losses will make the adjustment to the new situation even more difficult. Some children will experience difficulties at school during this period and it is important for parents and teachers to communicate with each other in order to help children through the difficulties. Sensitivity, support and reassurance will help the child feel understood and will indicate to them that the adults are aware of their feelings.

What are the mediating factors which can contribute to adaptation?

Our clinical experience (Gorell Barnes and Dowling, 1997; Dowling and Gorell Barnes, 1999) is confirmed by research findings (Richards, 1991; Rodgers and Pryor, 1998):

- Children need an explanation. They need to understand that although their parents can no longer live together they will remain interested in and responsible for them. Having an explanation will help children move on from the idea that they were responsible for the break up, or that if they try hard enough they might bring the parents back together.
- When children maintain good relationships with both parents, the negative effects of divorce are mitigated.

- Continuing conflict between the parents after divorce has a negative effect on children.
- Knowledge about the absent parent is beneficial even if there is no contact.
- Psychological well-being of parents: the quality of parenting is likely to diminish if parents are distressed and parent/child relationships will suffer. How well a parent adjusts has a significant impact on how well the child adjusts.

It may seem very difficult for parents when emotions are raw to try to find a cooperative way of making arrangements for the children and to keep in mind what is in their best interest, rather than continuing the battle. Children need to understand that it may be the end of the marriage, but not the end of the parent–child relationship.

The teenage years

As children grow older, the relationship with the parents changes and the peer group increases its importance. However, the break up of the family will have a powerful impact on the adolescent. Simons *et al.* (1996) found that adolescents in divorced families were significantly more involved in delinquent behaviour and early sex than those in intact families, regardless of the quality of the parents' marriage. On the interpretation of their findings they comment:

> This pattern of findings suggests that, in large measure, the relationship between parental divorce and adolescent problems is explained by the following causal sequence: marital disruption increases the probability that a woman will experience economic pressures, negative life events and psychological depression. Reductions in the quality of parenting, in turn, increase a child's risk for emotional and behavioural problems. (p. 20)

Their findings also suggest that 'The quality of father's parenting accounts for part of the link between family structure and child adjustment' (p. 213), and this is highlighted in the following example:

Doreen, mother of four children, felt quite depressed after her husand walked out in pursuit of a younger woman. She found it difficult to go out and had occasional panic attacks. She consulted her GP as she was concerned about the behaviour of three of her children. The two younger brothers (10 and 12) were disruptive at school and their older sister was getting into fights. The oldest of the girls had adopted a parentified role, looking after her mother and the house and as a result her school work and social life was suffering. During discussion with the mother it emerged that the father's contact with the children was very erratic and they felt very angry and let down by him.

Children's difficulties and family structure: divorce as a risk factor

Just as social structures are interconnected with social processes, it is important to examine the relationship between family structure, family processes and their relationship to children's chances of developmental difficulties.

Rodgers and Pryor (1998) in their comprehensive review of over 200 research studies linking parental separation and outcomes for children, have concluded that children of separated families compared with intact families:

- Tend to achieve less in socio-economic terms when they become adult than children from intact families.
- Are at increased risk of behavioural problems, including bed-wetting, withdrawn behaviour, aggression, delinquency and other antisocial behaviour.
- Tend to perform less well in school and to gain fewer educational qualifications.
- Are more likely to be admitted to hospital following accidents, to have more reported health problems and to visit their family doctor more often.
- Are more likely to leave school and home when young, and more likely at an early age to become sexually active; more likely to form a cohabiting partnership, to become pregnant; more likely to become a parent, or to give birth outside marriage.

- Tend to report more depressive symptoms and higher levels of smoking, drinking and other drug use during adolescence and adulthood.

Though the differences are clear, the authors stress that it *cannot be assumed* that parental separation is their underlying cause. 'The complexity of factors that impinge on families before, during and after separation indicates a *process* rather than a single *event* that merits careful examination' (p. 5).

These findings are confirmed by Simons *et al.* (1996):

> Our data suggest that divorce is an important risk factor for child adjustment problems. Although the majority of children show normal patterns of development regardless of their parents' marital status, children of divorce are significantly more likely to develop problems than those living with both parents. (p. 200)

However, they stress that: 'Although a risk factor increases the odds of a certain negative consequence, most people exposed to it do not suffer this ill effect' (p. 202).

In the chapters that follow, we consider what we know about aspects of family relationships which promote children's resilience and well-being. Our work with children and parents has been oriented towards identifying and promoting those factors in order to ameliorate the effects of divorce on children's mental health.

Summary

- Children need secure relationships with their caregivers in order to develop healthy emotional and social relationships.
- Children's wish for proximity, attention and responsiveness needs to be understood as a developmental expression of their needs.
- The most common source of children's anger is the frustration of their wish for love and care, and their anxiety abut parental availability.

- Divorce is an important risk factor for children's adjustment problems.
- Although a risk factor increases the odds of a certain negative consequence, it does not mean every one exposed to it will suffer the ill effect.

What helps children after separation and divorce

- An age-appropriate explanation for the family break-up.
- Absence of conflict between parents after divorce.
- Good relationships and easy contact with both parents.
- Knowledge about the absent parent, even if there is no contact.
- How well a parent adjusts has a significant impact on how well children adjust.

3

FAMILIES GOING THROUGH THE TRANSITIONS OF DIVORCE: RESEARCH FOCUS ON A CLINICAL SAMPLE

In this chapter we will introduce the families with whom we have worked over the last five years in the divorce research project, to show some of the complexities of life experience with which divorce and separation processes can be interwoven. The work described took place as part of a child and family mental health service in inner London. We have selected certain aspects of family culture, structure and organisational arrangements for all the families we have seen, and against this background we will set the clinical dilemmas and approaches discussed in Chapters 4 and 5.

Thirty families and 50 children aged from 4 to 15 sought help, either at the time of or following separation or divorce. The families came from mixed backgrounds, countries of origin and cultures. Countries of origin included South Africa, Argentina, Brazil, the Caribbean, Colombia, Cyprus, France, Holland, India, Iran, Ireland, Israel, the Lebanon, Malaysia, the UK and the USA. In over half the families we saw, one parent had been born outside the UK during their own lifetime (16 in all), and for 12 families this was true of both parents. The multicultural nature of the families reflects the changing nature of the population in many parts of the UK. For some couples the failure to develop a shared cultural meaning system was openly talked about as contributing to the differences between them, whereas in others the subject was not raised. The diversity in world view between man and woman, husband and wife was described by fathers and mothers as at times compounded by extreme differences within the belief systems of men and women in their different cultural backgrounds. In several families this dissonance was seen reflected at an intergenerational level, and as a result they had experienced themselves as disadvantaged and disapproved of by the parents of their partner. The ways in which the extended family, back home or in this country, was seen as a resource or an additional stress is described further below.

Gender differences in the divorce process

Hetherington, one of the foremost researchers on changes in families following divorce and remarriage, has suggested that just as the experiences of men and women in relation to marriage are so different that we should talk of 'his and hers' marriage, there may also be 'his and hers' divorce (Hetherington and Tryon, 1989). In her studies of mainly culturally coherent couples, women reported a longer period of dissatisfaction with their marriages prior to taking the decision to divorce than men. They also had divorce as an option in their minds for a longer period of time than their husbands. The men were often insensitive to their wives dissatisfaction and were surprised when the wish to divorce was voiced. A study of all divorces in one town in one year in Sweden, again from a culturally coherent background, found a similar gender pattern of dissatisfaction, with 80 per cent of divorces being initiated by the women (Wadsby, 1993).

Other studies have reported that men are much less accepting than women of the end of their marriages and may therefore experience greater distress after their wives have actually taken the step of separating (Hetherington and Tryon, 1989; Kiecolt Glaser et al., 1987). However, in our experience, suffering may be related to the experiences characterising the positions of 'leaver and left', rather than to gender itself. In thinking about divorce and the characteristics of emotional experience it becomes important to distinguish those who chose to initiate separation from those who experienced themselves as forsaken. A definition of 'leaver' or 'left' can become a key point in post-divorce definitions of 'self', and can be reinforced by legal disputes with allocation of 'penalty' points or 'damage' limitation awards.

When may individuals be in danger of becoming locked into a key 'definition' of themselves as 'leaver' or 'left' which subsequently may become disempowering as a self-description? How may such definitions need to change before cooperative parenting can develop? Leaver and left may have quite different experiences of sadness and relief, of fragmentation or increased well-being and of the return of self-esteem following the experience of living apart. Either may need to experience some of the emotions that are being held and expressed by their former partner for the couple's relationship to move on in more freeing ways.

In our group, half of the separations were initiated by women, against a quarter by men; of the remaining couples three agreed it had been a joint decision and the other couples had cohabited in diverse ways which had not involved forming one clear household together. The greatest single reason for separating given by women was violence. Eight women put violence as a primary reason for initiating divorce, while another five who reported on violent episodes placed their wish to divorce in a wider context of infidelity, drug and alcohol abuse, overbearing behaviour and financial insecurity. Other reasons given included the wish to develop careers unconstrained by their partner's views, financial unreliability in the male 'provider', or hostility to the children's fathers accompanied by a preference for living with another woman.

The greatest single reason given by men for initiating a separation was that they had fallen in love with another woman. Five of the fathers who initiated a divorce offered this explanation. Other reasons given by men included 'unreasonable behaviour' in a wife, and 'bad family choice' by father's parents and the extended family in the first place. Couples who took joint responsibility for the divorce, while angry with each other, did not lay the blame on either party singly. A few of the couples found it hard to make the move from living in one house to the next stage of reorganising their living arrangements apart, whether or not they had put the divorce in motion. People who were reluctant to negotiate changes expressed a number of profound fears: what would happen if the two of them moved apart, sadness at the thought of the break-up of the daily structures of family life as they knew them, anxiety about money, and anxiety about the effects on the children of the visible separation of their parents. Included in the fears expressed were their own doubts about the 'rightness' of divorce. 'It's like falling from grace!', as one father put it, 'going through the mire', as another said, and 'losing the codes by which life has been organised', expressed by several parents.

In the months that followed separation, the abilities of parents to adapt to being without the other varied widely, especially in the context of observing the reactions and emotions of the children. In our own minds, based on research across the Western world, the ability of mothers and fathers to establish a cooperative relationship was seen as an important predictive factor for the children's well-being. However, given the context of our work in a department that cares for the mental health dilemmas of adults as well as children, the psychological problems that parents reported were, not surprisingly, extensive and often got in the way of developing cooperative parenting.

Parents mental well-being

One-third of the women reported that they had been extremely depressed for periods of three months or more at some time during the divorce process. Five of these women had been left by their partners, two wished to leave the marriage but felt trapped by financial stalemate over selling the family home, and three had experienced violence. Other reported mental states included high anxiety and panic attacks (following some very violent episodes in the home), acute phobic behaviours and paranoid symptoms (which had pre-dated the separation), as well as general high levels of anxiety about how they would manage finance and the children. Nonetheless, all mothers but one seen by us continued to maintain a family home and the daily structure of the children's lives.

An example of the effect of maternal depression can be found in Joseph who was referred by his school for increasingly dreamy and inattentive behaviour. Anxieties were expressed about him being autistic or perhaps being of much lower intelligence than had been believed. On meeting his parents his behaviour was contextualised by the knowledge that his mother had been acutely depressed for at least six months She vividly described her inner state:

when my mind first started slipping, it was last year, I felt was a lost case... and I became very very depressed, I had, I had lost a lot of weight and I felt Richard [her husband] was just indifferent to everything... I was feeling like killing myself everyday; so if I had the courage I would have done, but every time I run to the children's picture, and I said what are they going to do, and then I'll cry and cry and cry and then I go back and ask for help... and I used to look at the children's' pictures, three together, and I used to say how could I do that to them. It would be a very coward attitude of mine to do that to them... I could do it to him, or to me but not to them.

Joseph's behaviour could then be linked to his concern for his mother. He was able to talk about his worries that his mother was very ill, that she might die; and he drew pictures of his parents separating as two ships colliding with the ends broken off and hungry sharks waiting for the passengers beneath. Work with Joseph's family, as with many others where parents are having hidden fights and children do not understand the process, involved the construction of explanations with his mother, his father and his two sisters in which he felt freed from being responsible for what was going on between his parents and which gave him a clearer idea of what the outcome would be for himself and his sisters.

Other studies report that divorced adults exhibit higher degrees of anger, anxiety and depression, antisocial and impulsive behaviour. They may also be at greater risk for suicidal behaviour. In our sample, fathers more often presented in an angry mode that disguised other emotional states. Four described being very depressed and one-third described underlying anxiety in relation to managing their lives without their wives and children. Other work has shown how divorced men and women (but men in particular) may experience disruptions in the functioning of their immune systems (Kiecolt and Glaser et al., 1987). While physical illness in parents was not an aspect reported to us, it is more likely to be shown in the context of general practice (see Chapter 9). Many parents reported an increase in alcohol intake, with at least three suffering severely from out-of-control drinking for a period of time. (In each of these families alcohol had previously presented itself as a problem at some point in the course of the partnership.)

Changes in finance and work patterns

In the months that follow the decision to separate and the initiation of the divorce processes themselves, many potentially stressful changes take place in the structures of the family world. The changes in financial arrangements often mean that homes have to be sold, or mortgages readjusted while one parent seeks a separate residence. Three couples seen by us were not able to manage this aspect of separation for some years after the decision to divorce had been taken. Overtly this was for reasons of finance, but ongoing emotional entanglements complicating the decision over whether to move were also described. Family interviews in which parents faced their children with their decision to leave home, sometimes involved long financial discussions which parents had previously been unable to undertake on their own. In one home an attempt was made to separate parental living arrangements by blocking up passageways and filling in doors, but this proved more provocative than useful. In five families the father retained the original home and mother moved out. In four of these the children moved between father and mother in formal or informal shared residence arrangements, and in two the parents had taken one child each. In five the original home was vacated by both sides of the family, and the children lived primarily with mother. In four families the original transition predated our meeting and we did not enquire, and in all other families the mother retained the matrimonial home.

Work patterns among the mothers changed relatively little in the context of divorce, although the amount of work many mothers were doing was increased by the parenting demands that devolved on them in the post-divorce period. Over one-third of the mothers were already in full-time employment and, of these, half had shared care with their former husbands in fairly equal ways. These were fathers who either retained one of their children when they separated from their wives, or maintained committed and emotionally highly-involved parenting following separation. None of these fathers had jobs involving regular 'office hours'. Three fathers whose former wives worked full-time increased their paternal involvement in the context of separation, creating intensive conflict which led to their gaining residence in two cases. Of the mothers who previously worked part-time, three took on additional jobs, declared or undeclared, in order to manage the increased financial burdens that separation entailed. These mothers therefore found they were managing increased work loads at the same time as managing rearranged routines for the children. Of the women who worked part-time, four took on higher training or education. Three mothers did not work outside the home and one woman gave up working altogether, preferring to recover from the anxiety created by a particularly violent divorce experience, and she retrained some years later.

For women, the context of stressed relationships with former spouses now learning to coparent in markedly different ways, often included economic as well as emotional conflict. Women more often expressed financial strain than men and responded by increased working hours, while men continued a former workload unchanged but learnt more about the emotional dimensions of combining work requirements with parenting. Mothers more often worked long hours in addition to managing more complex child-care juggling than fathers. Given the multiple tasks associated with this early change period, the child's point of view and their wishes for explanations and understanding of the changes taking place could be overlooked; the desire to get the structures working smoothly taking priority over establishing clearer communication patterns between parent and child. While much research has referred to this as 'a chaotic period' in family life, this was rarely the case in the families we saw, most parents keeping the daily structure of family life as well maintained as possible on behalf of children. Most women whose work hours increased involved others such as grandparents, neighbours, new partners or boyfriends and paid help of varying kinds to assist them, but some women whose families were not in this country bore the added strain alone.

Women's experiences of post-divorce mothering

An account of the mothers who have shared their experiences with us must include a recognition of the differences between them, before considering some of the common features of post-divorce 'mothering' that they expressed. Differences included money, education and employment opportunities, ethnicity and culture. Another series of differences lie in the social support offered by the extended family. Each of these differences provides a range of idiosyncratic discourses about the ways that the daily lives of mothers are made up, which alternate with the discourses about the changing role of fathers in their children's lives as well as their concerns about the children. However, all women had to deal with common issues around motherhood in the context of separating from the fathers of the children. What attitudes did they hold about how mothers should behave prior to separating and how did these ideas translate themselves into action in the context of post-separation changes in family life? How did they cope with the discrepancies between the ideals of motherhood and the realities they were experiencing? How did theories of good mothering that they themselves held influence the way they attempted to think about the changing family of which they were a part, and in particular of their children's needs?

Women talked about themselves, their former partners and their children along six main dimensions:

1. The pragmatics of everyday life (money, time, work, survival skills).
2. Psychological theorising about what was going on in the lives of different members of the family (their former partner's emotional state, the effect this was having on the children, the children's own states, the relationships between themselves and the children).
3. Issues of childrearing, whether to be more authoritarian or more permissive, power and control.
4. The ways in which their own childhood feelings were reactivated, both in relation to their relationship with their own children but also in the context of some of the relationships that they observed between their own children and their parents.
5. Wider relational issues to do with their own families of origin and the way these relationships were changing for their children following the parental separation.
6. Contact arrangements and their effects on children.

An approach to discussing changes

In thinking about divorce and its social impact on women and 'motherhood', a wider social lens was taken to discuss the variations in mothering within which women could describe and analyse themselves. Bearing in mind the lowered self-esteem that often accompanies divorce, it seemed essential to our work in developing better coparenting and family arrangements that no parent should consider themselves and their self-defined 'shortcomings' as deviant. The focus we took was on 'resilience' rather than on pathology. While dominant and often idealised views about 'good motherhood' continually recurred, it could also be acknowledged in the conversations that we do not have dominant ideas about the good motherhood of divorce. Personal constructions can be placed against more idealised and public versions within a joint framework of awareness that public versions of good parenting often do not have any real knowledge about the post-divorce dilemmas that a particular mother describes. Women were therefore encouraged to think in what ways they were contributing to the store of knowledge that is growing. In this way we thought together as participants in a social process and not only at the level of their individual suffering in the context of a stressful life event (Gorell Barnes, 1998).

This work also applied to widening the lens with parents and children. Such talking often helped to identify resources, or ways of handling issues that the children were raising from a position of strength rather than of guilt. For example, a discussion with sons about a father being told to leave by a mother, while also working with the hurt of loss for all involved, could move from the position of 'women as unkind and therefore needing to be paid back', as formerly defined by the boys, to a wider discussion about the effects of drugs and alcohol on a man (their father), on behaviour, and on love and relationships. Similarly a wife's inability to fulfill her husband's expectations of a 'good wife' as witnessed in a row by her children could be redefined in a wider social discussion about the changing expectations held between husbands and wives about what men do and what women do, and how men and women disagree as observed within the lives of the children's friends as well as their own family.

Men's experiences of post-divorce fathering

Many of the men confronted with the removal of their children from their households felt devastated about the extent of the changes in the daily rhythm of their lives. As mentioned earlier in the chapter there was a marked variety in the kinds of fathering offered within the children's weekly pattern. A small number of children (three families) saw their father most days even though they lived with their mothers, and a further 12 families saw their fathers most weeks. At the opposite end of the spectrum three fathers dropped out of their children's lives altogether, three who lived overseas saw them less than once a month or during holidays, and a number of children saw their fathers 'several' times a year. Two sets of children switched their home to live with their fathers after a period with their mothers. Three of the families had split arrangements for different children with three children remaining with their father while their sibling went to live with their mother. This broke down in one instance and the child returned to his mother and stepfather. One couple took turns to look after the children, depending on which of them was in employment.

For about a quarter of the men their construction of 'fatherhood' or 'patriarchy' was severely challenged by the divorce. Two of these fathers removed themselves from contact with their former wives. One man struggling to remain involved expressed his puzzlement in a strangely archaic way:

Alfie: [Talking disapprovingly about a friend who had also divorced] ... He's completely pulled back from the patriarchal role ...

GGB: Suppose you let the patriarchal role go for a year, what do you think would happen?

Alfie: Well, first of all, I'm just not absolutely sure that I can. I don't know how one can pluck out 'dad' and replace with 'parent'.

Sybil: [Mother] Do you need to pluck out dad?

GGB: Why is 'dad' and 'Patriarch' the same?

Sybil: There's lots of aspects of your relationship that are 'dad' that are not 'patriarch' [lists them] I think they're the majority ... But there's still that 'yck' area ... at least I consider it 'yck' ... maybe I don't like the word 'patriarchal'.

Alfie: I suppose I've just got to give up the idea of being the Boss ... [mother laughs and father continues] ... I suppose you effectively gave that idea up when you filed for divorce.

Sybil: Yes, I just think 'boss' is not on any more ... dated.

The importance for fathers of developing attachments to their children has been argued by many child development researchers, themselves men and fathers (Lamb, 1997). However, the placing of this attachment within frameworks of skills relevant to parenting in the context of post-divorce living may simultaneously require the development of new reflections about the meanings involved in the tasks of parenting, about the nature of childhood and development, and upon new more flexible constructions of 'man' and 'father':

> And I mean, to me, a father's role, from the sort of society I come from, was the sort of the tough, bluff, let the mum look after the kids sort of thing, you know, and I'll go down to the ale house and that sort of . . . mmm . . . And that's not the sort of role that I'm playing, or have played. It's mum and dad role that I'm playing. You know I find that instead of saying now look, get up, you're going to be okay, be a man, I've got to go over and cuddle him.

Many divorced fathers, whether taking primary care of their children, or operating from a non-residential position can initially feel confused or apprehensive about their parenting role (Seltzer, 1991; Hart, 1994; Bratley, 1996). Studies that have looked in depth at what fathers say about their own experiences find that many of them report being uncertain about what to do during visits, particularly with young children. Most of the children in our study were of school age and already had well-established relationships with their fathers. Questions were more often around how a fathers' role should change, than whether he would develop one at all. However, the degree of panic many fathers showed at the relationship with their children getting less, indicated what an essential component of their own development was invested in the lives of their children, and this was a valuable way-in to thinking about the changing nature of their relationships.

The relationship with the children's mother remains a key factor in father's successful maintenance of contact. Different studies in different parts of the Western hemisphere show that when legal wrangling with former wives is stressful, when fathers feel they have little control over court decisions or what will happen to their children, or when conflict is ongoing, they are less likely to stay involved or to pay child support (Arditti and Allen, 1993; Hetherington, 1992; Kruk, 1992). Seltzer and Brandreth (1994) in the USA and Simpson in the UK (Simpson, McCarthy and

Walker, 1995), have noted how resident mothers act as gatekeepers after divorce, potentially controlling fathers' contact with children. Our own study bore this out to a marked degree and raised the ongoing question of how men can learn to parent their children in ways that are not organised by the value system of the spouse from whom they are now trying to establish separate lives, while still retaining their goodwill.

There is some evidence that the first post-divorce year may be an especially important period for the establishment of patterns of father involvement. High conflict and low cooperation at this time can interfere with new parenting patterns being developed. If a positive relationship is not established during the first post-divorce year, father and children may each adjust to their loss, and future involvement becomes less likely and less important to either's well-being (Ahrons and Miller, 1993). However recent work in the UK (Simpson, McCarthy and Walker, 1995) suggests that fathers may struggle to stay involved over much longer periods and that interventions organised towards helping them with contact can be worthwhile many years following separation. As in Chapter 1, we would prefer to emphasise the variety in the experiences men shared with us in relation to the development of their fathering roles rather than to agree with a unitary definition. We suggest four different patterns of involvement in relation to the small sample of fathers described in this study:

1. Fathers who responded to their wives' decision to separate with outrage and withdrawal. These fathers self-divided into two groups, in this first of which they withdrew altogether, though writing angry letters asserting their own rightful cause. Only two fathers behaved in this way.
2. Fathers who responded with outrage, but struggled to retain contact with their children in spite of their own difficult life circumstances. This group contained three fathers who had serious problems of alcohol or drug abuse, and two who had serious business difficulties to contend with that had left them in financial hardship.
3. Fathers whose involvement increased in the context of post-divorce fathering. Ten of the fathers moved strongly into what were initially intermittent but increasingly strong commitments to their children.

4. Fathers who had always been as involved, or more strongly involved, in the upbringing of their children as their partners. Five of the fathers we saw came into this category. These men were also seen by the children's mothers as 'coparents' from before the decision to separate, although the degree of their involvement was seen by some of the women as posing some problems to the children. These concerns were generally around fathers' over-dependence on the children for their own emotional fulfilment. (This gender-related anxiety about men's' involvement with their children is discussed further in Chapter 4, since it raises interesting questions about how such a judgement can be discussed with a parent, on behalf of a young person's development over time.) One father found it very difficult to accept his daughter's wish to spend more time with her mother when this was developmentally appropriate. He wanted to adhere rigidly to what he saw as a 'fair share' of their eldest daughter.

Relationship changes following separation: losses, additions and emotions

Parents themselves described the processes of change surrounding the divorce in very different ways. Some processes such as violence or ongoing anger expressed through rough solicitor's letters, angry telephone calls and lengthy faxes were highly visible, whereas other aspects of relationship change came into focus more gradually, or remained concealed in ways that were to the children's' disadvantage. As the families we worked with were constantly 'in transition' we will give an account of the variety of relationship changes that children and parents experienced during the years that we knew them in Chapter 7. Some of these were experienced as positive changes, but some new relationships were experienced by parents as an added loss, or by children as further complications of attachment or loyalty. Most families were seen over a period of between one and two years, and we followed up the first 20 families we saw over three years, in some cases to five years.

Initially three times as many mothers as fathers lived on their own with the children. Four mothers had a regular or living-in boyfriend, three mothers had undeclared but subsequently declared lesbian live-in partnerships, two sets of parents who separated lived on their own but took a child each, and one woman moved to live with her mother.

Initially 11 fathers lived on their own, and 13 lived with a woman friend without children, thus introducing the children to a new relationship very soon after the parents had separated. Four fathers moved into a relationship where they became part-time 'parent' figures to their partner's children, thus introducing children to the idea of new stepsibling relationships. In addition, this required children to change their ideas about their father, seeing him with another set of children with whom he was in a semi-parental relationship. One father joined a second family with children he had created concurrently while living with the family who referred themselves to us; one had a sexually explicit relationship with a women who worked in the house for him but did not formally live with him.

Over three years, patterns changed further. Only three of the mothers continued to live alone, the others having either a regular boyfriend or living-in partner, and two having borne a child by the new relationship. Through the relationships developed by fathers, seven sets of children had acquired either new stepsiblings or half-siblings. Thus in addition to the process of going through the changes incurred by the break-up of the original nuclear family, *all children seen had over two years been through the experience of one or both parents acquiring a new adult relationship*, and one-third had also become acquainted with new stepbrother/sister or half-brother/sister figures of varying degrees of closeness. The experience of family transition therefore included complex changes in expected sets of connection, if not of attachment to new relationships, both with adults and sometimes with 'stranger' children. Children's concerns about the meaning of these new relationships often formed a powerful part of their interviews with one of us, or subsequent interviews with their parents.

Extended-family support

How did distance or proximity affect the way that parents felt connected to their extended families, seeing them as a resource for themselves or the children? For those parents whose own parents lived in another country, the way in which the extended family might nonetheless act as a resource was equally divided into those who continued to use their families in positive and helpful ways, and those who did not. Half the parents kept in regular touch with their wider family, through long telephone calls, through grandparental visits to this country or through visits to grandparents for holidays; as well as children visiting grandparents for holidays on their own while parents continued to work. The range of emotional relationships between parents and grandparents varied from warm and positive to highly ambivalent. For the other half of the parents, contact with their own parents had become much more uncertain and was not considered a resource.

For mothers, reasons given included their own powerful emotional feelings arising from negative experiences in their childhoods which were rearoused in the context of visits with their own children. Such uncomfortable feelings as of having been criticised when young were often amplified by the current experience of ongoing critical comments about the divorce itself, or about their own current parenting of their children as well as witnessing their grandparents inability to treat their own children as children. Additional reasons for not relating to parents included active unkindness or neglect in childhood, the turning of a 'blind eye' to sexual abuse from a male relative in mother's childhood, and patriarchal views held by senior male relatives, from which a daughter, now as a mother, was trying to escape.

Where grandparents were present in this country they were only slightly more likely to be regarded as a resource, since of the 13 mothers and fathers who had parents available only half (of both mothers and fathers) regarded them as family they could turn to. More than half the mothers who had their mothers geographically available to them and saw them on a regular basis also expressed highly ambivalent feelings in these relationships with their mothers. Fathers were more likely to make use of their parents since seven out of the nine fathers who had a family in another country, and nine out of 13 men with parents in this country, kept closely in touch with them.

For fathers, a different range of intergenerational relationships was shown in their accounts of their parents. More men described their relationships with their parents primarily as a resource or a commitment; a 'bond' between themselves and their parents which they wanted to maintain. Parents were therefore more often talked about as 'parents' and only in a secondary way as grandparents. This may have reflected the social position men visiting their parents were more often likely to find themselves in, since more of them visited their own parents on their own, while their children were in mother's care in addition to taking the children on visits to their grandparents. It may also have reflected an expectation that some, as men, would look after their parents when they were older, independent of their role as a father to children. This closer relationship between men and their families was also described as contributing to tensions in the formerly married couple, particularly where a wife viewed the alliance between a husband and his own family as offering a closeness which in some way excluded her; or where she saw it as diminishing her own position by requiring her to defer to parental expectations in ways she would not have chosen to support or by which she felt directly criticised. This included putting up with thinly-disguised racist comments within the family, in two cases, and homophobic comments for two of the three mothers who subsequently chose to live in lesbian partnerships. One professional Indian woman had to support a mother-in-law's position and rights in the household at the expense of her own happiness to a degree beyond what she found culturally acceptable to herself. Three women experienced themselves as forced into a subsidiary position in relation to the importance of family business requirements, where the son had entered as a partner into the family business.

Since so many parents had moved from one country to another or married into another culture, we were interested to see in what ways parents themselves related the experiences of moving country or culture to the increased stresses or tensions in the marriage. In a third of the families, parents related the dilemmas within their marriages as connected to the characteristics of cultures from which they came or into which they had married. This included such qualities as expressiveness and 'temperament', style of communication, definitions of what men and women may expect of one another in relation to particular aspects of role, cultural practices such as family meals or the amount of time to be spent with extended family and friends, as well as beliefs about child rearing. In three marriages of mixed ethnicity the children's skin colour had itself become a matter for argument or comment within the extended families.

In a number of the families characterised by violence, cultural differences had played a part in extremely different ideas between husband and wife about their required roles and behaviours. For example the cultural requirements to honour a husband's mother and father; the harsh disciplinary beliefs of a man reared in an upwardly mobile family in the Far East; rebellion against the hierarchical and chauvinistic expectations in the family of origin of a woman from the Southern Mediterranean which she believed had preconditioned her to tolerate similar behaviour in her husband; the religious requirements which prescribed certain expectations of behaviour within the marriages of a number of couples. Paradoxically, it was the qualities of difference in cultures that had attracted some couples to each other initially, that subsequently became seen as something they were trying to get away from.

The kinds of referrals made for children?

Referrals amongst the children as a whole fell into three broad categories:

1. Those primarily referred for help with problems emerging due to unresolved disputes between parents.
2. Those who had symptoms that were worrying to their parents, which had not necessarily been connected to undiscussed issues arising in the divorce process.
3. Those who were causing concern in school.

Unresolved disputes between parents included opposing and 'irreconcilable' views about the different ways they wanted their children to manage their daily lives; or the belief that the child could not be managed because the other parent was 'impossible'. Such passionate statements characterised many of the opening statements made by parents. More idiosyncratic presentations included the denial by a father that one of the children was his own, and therefore a wish to cease contact; acute disarray in post-divorce arrangements due to manic-depressive illness and business failure; alcohol or drug addiction; and concern about specific aspects of contact arrangements where a parent was moving to live outside the UK. Less visible breakdown of former good family functioning included extreme sadness in mothers who had been left by their partners, often accompanied by an inability to be clear with the children about what was happening in relation to the separation and the imminent or actual divorce. A number of referrals additionally included issues to do with profound clashes between parents and their subsequent partner about how the children were to be handled.

Violence between parents and between parents and children

Children who had witnessed parents being violent with one another showed a range of different symptoms. Thirteen were boys and seven were girls, and two girls began to remember violence and abuse some time after initial referral. Boys' behaviour included night terrors and bed-wetting, shyness and nervousness, surliness and rudeness to their mother, verbal abuse and hitting or attacking their mother, and in one case attacking the father. In over half the families a specific child was reported by parents as doing less well in school, even though siblings might be doing as well as before. In only three cases were the referrals specifically connected to a schools anxiety about a child doing 'less well' at school. Such concerns ranged from lower key 'less able performance', to expulsion from several schools prior to referral. Girls from the same families where violence was part of the parental pattern were more likely to talk of sadness than of anger, and to show psychosomatic or phobic symptoms. In no case did a girl report being hit by her father, although boys from the same families had been hit on a number of occasions. We noted also that girls, who had not been hit, more often retained an even-handed or more impartial view of their fathers, staying in touch with their own positive feelings about him when their brothers seemed unable to do so.

In no case where children had not witnessed violence between parents did they hit or attack a parent themselves.

Children who had witnessed violence in a relationship that was balanced by witnessing other more cooperative aspects of a long term coparenting relationship after divorce, were able to talk about fights between parents while their parents were in the room (during family interviews with the two of us). However, where there had been violence followed by a father's disappearance from the scene, children did not want to talk about this in front of their mothers. We also found that young children talked more easily with their parents in the room, while those over seven preferred to talk with an adult on their own. The longer-term impact of violence on both women and children is discussed more fully in Chapter 6.

Children's own concerns

What are the issues that concern children when they learn about their parents separating and take on board the fact that things will never be the same again? It is first of all important to remember that children assimilate changes over varying periods of time, depending on their ages, their cognitive abilities, the knowledge available from their peer group in relation to parental break-up, and the degree of clarity between the parents themselves. Children have to find ways of making sense of their parents' conflicting views about why the divorce is happening, often accompanied by very different stories of who is to blame. They are usually only given partial information about what is going on, and often they are reluctant to ask for information in case what they find out is frightening. Sometimes they only learn through what they see, and have to make their own deductions about parental rows and unhappiness. Young children, in particular, are often unable to give meaning to what they see happening in terms of any former ideas about family change. Divorce itself, for example, may not mean to a child that his parents will not live together again and many children retain this wish in the face of their parents' believing they have made the meaning of events clear. The family climate of uncertainty often leads to the child trying to take charge of things in their own mind. The belief that they can hold the parents together has been expressed by many of the younger children seen in the study. 'I can bring them together again – I know I can – you wait and see', was a belief stated openly by at least four of the young boys. Feelings of power and powerlessness alternate, and powerlessness may spread to other aspects of their lives. Their own ability to be competent in relation to their

age and developmental stage may be undermined by their preoccupation with what is going on at home.

Young girls often expressed a wish to keep things together by
showing caretaking behaviour. Anna was five when her divorced
parents brought her to the Clinic because they were worried
about her adjustment to school and were concerned about the
effect of their divorce on her. Anna had already experienced a
number of transitions in her family, including the loss of close
friends of her mother who had died. At the first interview, Anna
busied herself in the session constantly. She rushed around, tidy-
ing up toys, pouring glasses of water, trying to look after the therapist and being very busy making pretend cups of coffee. In the
following extract, one of us (ED) is exploring her experience of
her parents' separation.

Anna: They always argue.
ED: That must be quite difficult for you to manage?
Anna: That's not really my fault. It's their fault.
ED: Of course it isn't your fault. But it must have felt at times that it
        was your fault.

And further on in the interview

ED: How long ago did mummy and daddy split up?
Anna: Fifteen years.
ED: It seems such a long time.
Anna: No, just three months. Just three months.

And further on in the interview:

Anna: When they don't live together. When my mummy and daddy
        don't live together, I really get upset.
ED: How do you show you are upset?
Anna: I am not upset today, or anything like that. Daddy's not cross
        with me any more and I try to always be good.
ED: Why was he cross with you?
Anna: He is never cross with me.

It was extremely difficult for Anna to come to terms with the fact
that her parents had decided to live apart and that it was still
going to be possible to be loved and liked by both of them. Because

the father did not want to split up, the end of his contact visit was particularly painful both for him and for Anna and her younger brother. From her mother's point of view, the contact was irregular and erratic and she never knew where she stood. There were very different beliefs about child-rearing and this caused considerable friction. Part of the work was to bring these differences into the meetings for the couple to discuss, so that they could agree on a way of managing the children that did not involve them in their ongoing conflict and differences. Over time, this allowed Anna to stop feeling she was the one who held things together by looking after everyone.

Conflicts of loyalty

Children may worry about one or both of their parents during separation and divorce, and once a parent has moved out of the house their loyalties about how to place themselves inevitably become conflicted, as in the following comments by Bob (on choosing):

> I was watching this programme 'Family Matters' and in the year 2000 there are going to be about 2½ million parents split up and the children are going to be ... could be told to choose, and then they could think ... Oh I'll want my mum and then they could think oh my dad will think 'they don't love me' and then they could go to the dad and the mother could think ... And what I don't like is that they could go to the mother and then think maybe they should love their dad more ... Or their mother ...

We have found that children as young as eight are well able to voice their uncertainty about the effect of their own love of one parent on the other. In addition they may be frightened about the way a parent behaves when they visit the other parent, since the behaviour may be jealous or vengeful. In this context they may hide their own feelings and uncertainties and adapt to what they feel is required of them. They are faced with the task of making sense of each parent, and knowing that each parent is part of them, struggling with how to integrate the very disparate sets of views they encounter. This process is made more difficult when their parents actively disqualify 'badmouth' one another in front of the children, or try to engage them in taking sides. 'My solicitors said that your mother was the maddest woman he had ever seen', or 'only your father would be stupid enough to think that he could put a child in that risky situation and get away with it'.

Worries about parents

When parents themselves may not be coping very well they are not always able to distinguish children's needs from their own. Nor do they always present good ways of coping for their children to imitate. We have found this to be so particularly where parents have adopted high-tension strategies in which violence is seen as an option, or, alternatively, strategies that are based on suppressing any discussion of what is going on. Where parents fight out in the open and try and get arrangements as clear as possible for the children, they are then able to develop models of how to think about the way their lives are henceforth going to be divided. However, their heads may become crowded with arguments and 'logical' reasoning, each series of arguments sounding 'reasonable' in its own right but impossible to manage if both are placed side by side (the same experience can happen in the process of mediating disputes when professionals experience themselves as divided between streams of irreconcilable 'righteousness') as each parent describes their position. In such circumstances children may develop a variety of protective devices designed to keep a safe place in their minds (heads, imagination, lives). These include day-dreaming, withdrawal into computer games, endless watching of TV or videos, or overactivity such as taking care of imaginary families or friends

In the chapters that follow we describe some of the work we have done with parents and children, and then go on to link our work within the Clinic to work in schools and primary health care settings.

4

WORKING WITH PARENTS AND THEIR CHILDREN: A FOCUS ON PARENTS

As the family begins to engage with the experience of separation and change, each person from their different position and role experiences individual stress, in addition to the collective stress that affects everyone. In recognising the separate stresses that led to separate stories we found it useful to work with individual family members as well as different combinations of family relationships. The goals of helping the parents move forward with their changing relationship in ways that took a positive account of the children's point of view remained central. However, allowing individuals to tell the story of the lead-up to the present situation from their point of view, without the editing that the presence of other family members might incur, became an essential part of the work. Where the divorce involved other sexual liaisons this process always involved a series of questions around 'how much should I/we tell the children'; but similar concerns about parent/child boundaries arose in relation to issues like violence, sexual dissatisfaction, and worries such as debt or mental illness, from which parents felt children should be protected. As children become entangled with parental disputes and loyalty issues it also proved useful to see different children with a particular parent to free them from some of the conflicted stories in which they were caught up, or to enlarge the information from which they had made deductions that were wrong and which were causing them unnecessary anxiety.

As discussed in Chapter 1, divorce and family reordering is accompanied by many other life changes affecting both parents and children. The external changes which may be losses for children, such as changes in home, possibly in school and neighbourhood, may be experienced as a relief by parents who have arrived at the decision that a change in their lives is what they are seeking. They may therefore fail to recognise the effects these losses are having on the children. For parents who have not sought a change, transitions may be experienced as losses in ways that reverberate with the children's experience, so that the parent is poorly equipped to help the children to deal with the changes by which they themselves are feeling oppressed.

As family therapists we normally take the family as the primary unit of our work, also looking at the wider social network with which different members are involved and relating to this where the family think it would be useful. In the family itself we focus on the relationships between different members and on trying to find ways of helping the communications to improve. It became apparent in our early clinical work with families in transition, that following a parental decision to separate it was very difficult for children's voices and the different perspective of children on the processes taking place in the family to get a hearing. It also became evident that children were often in a loyalty bind between their parents, and the different stories that they told about the processes leading up to the separation and the separation and divorce themselves. This made it difficult for children to talk about their own stress and concerns arising from the experience of parental separation while they were in the presence of one or both parents. In the course of the project we therefore developed ways of working with all the relationships in the family in different combinations. This allowed the very differing views about what was going on and the effects of one person's behaviour on another to emerge. Children's voices in particular could be heard in ways that influenced their parents and led to changes in the ways that arrangements were subsequently made for the children. The work with children is described in detail in Chapter 5. In this chapter we address the work with parents and the family work as a whole.

Given that adults, at a time when they are themselves under severe stress, have to make the decisions which have both short-term and possibly long-term effects, we were keen to make use of the research which has established protective factors for children and to operationalise these where possible. This led to us developing questions about changes in family life which we asked of both parents and children, more formally in a research-based interview, as well as more informally in the course of the work we did together. Studies from both the USA and Australia, as well as those in the UK, have shown that in the short term children from divorcing families show more difficulties at school, have increased health problems including a range of psychosomatic problems, and have an increased negative self-image and low self-esteem. In developing with a parent or a child questions about their own images of themselves, the family and the child's daily life we might therefore explore the changes in some detail. For example: in what ways do children and parents see differences in the family developing in the context of transitions, and what do each of them think about these? Which parent has the child been closest to on a daily basis and which of his parents does he now see less of? How are the arrangements for contact being planned to take his own attachments to either parent into account, not just the parents' views of 'what is fair'? How much of the larger family will he now be cut off from, and what arrangements will be thought of for him not to lose those connections with grandparents, uncles and aunts? The exploration is around the former 'balance' of a child's life and how it has changed and will continue to change. Parents also need help in considering in what ways the multiple adjustments required of children in the context of change may for a time prevent other exploration or learning from taking place at the usual rate. In many cases it has been valuable to establish contact with the children's schools.

Orientation of our work on behalf of the children

The conditions which are more likely to make it possible for children to manage this particular life-transition well have been summarised in Chapter 2 as follows:

- Where children maintain good relationships with both parents the potential negative effects of divorce are mitigated.

- Continuing conflict between parents after divorce has a negative effect on children. Any work that can bring about change in reducing conflict and diminish the involvement of the child in conflict is likely to be useful for the child's short-term well-being and long-term development and self-esteem.
- Where children are able to talk openly about the processes of change that affect their lives they are more likely to develop coping strategies themselves. This has been seen as a major contributor to resilience in childhood.

A family story in which both parents concur

In the context of our own experience of hearing the radically different and often conflicting stories that parents told about their marriages and cohabitations we decided that helping the parents to provide a narrative, however thin, in which there is a positive story line about the life of the family prior to the decision to separate would be one way towards helping the child recognise that two storylines could coexist without him having to side with either one of them. These stories should usually include some ideas about how mummy and daddy got together and used to love each other, but how people change in the course of living. This may involve ideas about human uncertainty, as well as the importance of different kinds of loving and a distinction between parental love and couple's love.

Freeing the children from personal blame

This will be discussed further in the next chapter from the child's point of view. In working with parents distinctions had to be made continually between what they professed, which was an awareness that the children were not to blame, and other messages of anger, of reproach and sometimes of straightforward accusation which led the child to feel as though it was their fault that the parental predicament was as it was.

Constructing new models of relationship between parents and children

In talking with parents and children together, parents often had to learn from their children how life was now different for them. This could mean that a parent was challenged to think about questions that they had not previously addressed, and talk with their children about how they were going to think about these questions, and respond to them.

How we worked

Many of the parents referred were already living separately, so we began by inviting the parent with whom the child(ren) had residence (which was usually the mother), and then asked for permission to contact the parent who lived away from home. Unless a parent had disappeared we always stated that our work was to promote the child's best interests, which involved both of their parents and obtained permission to make contact with the other parent during the initial meeting. Each of the parents was seen on their own on at least two occasions so that their stories about the marriage break-up and their views about how the children's future should be managed between them could be understood as fully as possible by one of us, with a recognition of all the differences these stories involved.

For many of the fathers it was the first opportunity they had had to tell their story. The children were usually seen at least twice without parents, on their own or with their brothers or sisters. We then worked in the following combinations, discussing and exchanging differences of view about what was going on and opening up questions for the family to clarify or explore further. We saw father and mother together wherever this was possible and each parent with their children. On a number of occasions we saw the whole family together to pull out the differences that had previously been hidden but that were contributing to confusion in the children.

In spite of their own disagreements with former partners, parents usually remain willing to help their children along agreed lines. However, experience taught us that in the acute aftermath of separation or divorce, where feelings continue to run higher than the voices of reason, there is a conflict between the parent's own needs and their ability to think about the children's needs. Redressing the balance and helping the parents attend to the children's needs becomes a crucial aspect of the therapeutic work. Mourning the loss of the former family 'the family as it was' is often something the children are able to voice, which the parents either do not wish to hear, or may themselves be defended against hearing because they too are finding the losses surprisingly painful. Moving to the different positions of coparents but no longer sexual or even companionate partners is both complex and often exhausting, and takes time. We found that we had underestimated the amount of time we would need to give professionally. The number of sessions families required to achieve some change of position that satisfied them varied from six sessions to over three years of monthly meetings.

Ambiguities in couples' relationships following separation

In thinking about the ambiguities in the relationships between couples who were formerly married or cohabiting over time, and who are now trying to continue a coparenting relationship, we have found it important to try to understand how each person is making sense of the inner images of the family they are leaving behind. Each partner carries an idea of their 'family' in their head. There may be key aspects of family living as it used to be, when the family was going well, that both adults and children may find it important to identify as an ongoing part of their own 'core' self, things they want to acknowledge and incorporate (Gorell Barnes, 1991). Sometimes this involves open expression of sorrow at facing the ending of the marriage and saying goodbye to the intimacy of family life. Betty, for example, mourned the lack of day-to-day sharing: 'I miss that terribly, and I miss when I read things in the papers...I mean, its like a loss, I think oh, that would amuse Philip.'

Sometimes, however, a parent may only hold fast to a fixed negative image of the other and the relationship they have had with them. If they can only hold onto the bad things it is likely to be detrimental to any future relationship the child may have with the other parent, as well as to the way the child thinks about that parent as a part of himself (see Chapter 7 for a further discussion). In such circumstances we have found it important to help divorcing parents talk through negative images of one another and find some positive images to balance them. The child is then freer to hold onto their own relationship with the other parent in the reordered family arrangements, rather than being put in the postion of having to defend one parent while in the presence of the other. For couples with a long history of high conflict we have found that in order to be freed from ongoing patterns of competitive parenting, which involves disqualifying the other parent, no significant change can be made without some sorrow being expressed over the way the relationship has gone wrong, accompanied by some recognition that things were once good.

We hazard a belief that there has to be some mutuality of purpose in the parenting couple, however minimal, before they can coparent successfully over time. A shift in focus is required away from each parent being preoccupied with whether they are right, towards joint concerns and good intentions for the children. Using the 'best interests' of the child, a principle embodied in the Children Act 1989 as a focus for discussion, has often helped parents shift from a self-centred to a more children-centred position.

Following a separation there is often a period in which each parent still acts as though the other parent were the same, as though the child was the same, and as though they themselves were unchanged. However, each adult slowly reformulates their own guiding principles for living, reconstructs their own networks of friends and support, and begins to follow pathways that have inbuilt differences from the person they were when they were living together with the other parent. These differences extend and amplify, and may become increasingly divergent as each partner finds their own feet and picks up their lives. As couples change they are often surprised to find how different the 'other' has become. This experience will to some degree also be true for all children, although for some, changes can be much more extreme than others.

Parents' relationships with their children

The relationship between parents and their children is of paramount importance to the newly emerging individual identity of adults following a marital break-up. Parents find themselves painfully vulnerable to their children's views of them. Children's observations about their behaviour and daily living habits can interpenetrate with their own self-esteem with a raw sensitivity. Some of the pain and fight following separation and divorce in long-term relationships involving children work against cooperation at complex levels. Fighting about money and children can often be defences against painful feelings of loss, and the agenda of 'looking after children' may not be separable for many years from the unfinished agenda between the couple. Rarely can one system of negotiations be unaffected by the inequalities experienced either way in relation to access to money, to goods and to children. A sense of unfairness may work against the emotional evenness that successful coparenting requires. As one couple whose marriage was characterised by both passion and violence said about their acrimonious contact disputes three years after the divorce:

Don: I feel the hidden agenda over Bob is from Jane to me. If I get involved in thinking with her about how to handle him it may open up something inadvisable. It may have reverberations which will lead us back into the mire.

Jane: Its not difficult for us to do things to one another . . . I become confused and start to fragment. I know I should have got over it years ago . . . I like Don a lot more now which makes it easier. It's been very difficult getting over him. I still feel very tied to him. I never had a period of saying 'that's over that's done' I still have confusion when I see him or spend time with him.

Don: A consuming fog settles between us very quickly . . . its a lack of instinctive information which becomes difficult. When you are together and having a bad time . . . there are still certain advantages in it . . . kinds of communication . . . codes which are set up so you are forewarned of things and can set up ways of sorting it out. If you split up but carry on with the kids you don't have those instinctive codes any more. People are having experiences elsewhere and the codes have changed.

It is also hard for parents to take on board the way children themselves change in relation to their ideas about their parents, and to their own lives. For example, Linda, aged 11, having had years of being shared equally between her parents, was beginning to want to spend more time with her mother. Her mother had become more connected to the preoccupations of her 11-year-old daughter and they were enjoying shopping trips and other activities together. This caused great resentment in her father who found it very difficult to give up some of his time with Linda.

Improving communication between parents and children

Children in the Exeter study (Cockett and Tripp, 1994), reported that they sometimes had to suppress talking to one parent about enjoying time with the other, or had been asked by one parent to keep something secret from a former partner in the ongoing context of contact visits. Only one in five children were reported as being able to talk freely about one parent in front of the other. Many did not feel free to talk about the divorce and about changes in family life. The study of young adults who had grown up in reordered families referred to earlier (Gorell Barnes *et al.*, 1998) showed that high degrees of silence had also been maintained into adult life. Many of the respondents said that even now they would feel the subject of the 'other parent' was taboo. As one young woman whose mother had left said, 'I'd have to ask my father things, and I don't think, I should imagine if I ever asked about her, he'd just completely blank the issue, he wouldn't talk about it. Or he'd get very cross with me, I can imagine him getting cross about that'. Another young woman for whom the inter-parental conflict had never ceased 20 years after the divorce, said ... 'I think a parent should never forget that the child has two parents, the original parents. My mother totally cut my father off from her and I felt she wanted me to do the same as well, but they were still my mother and father'.

It is well-known that anger makes communication difficult, and we discuss some of the effects of anger and violence on children and the ways in which we attempted to work with these very strong emotions in parents in Chapter 6. However, we have found that it is not only high-conflict emotion that makes communication difficult, but also emotion that is buried and that leads to silence, the denial that the separation is taking place or the erasing of memory of a parent who has gone by ceasing to bring him into the daily conversations of the family. A key function of therapeutic interviews can be to challenge such silences, and to help the parent with whom the child is living to make it permissible and possible for the parent who has gone to have a legitimised place in their minds.

Initially, a lack of clarity about the nature of parental arrangements related to parents' own uncertainty about whether a marriage is ended or not characterised a number of the lives of children in our study. Children showed their preoccupation by failing at school. A parent who has been left, or who is experiencing having been cheated and who is suffering deeply, may prefer to leave things unclear with their children in the hope that the balance of the marriage will revert to how it formerly was. As one mother, Gita, who was trying to make sense of the fact that her husband was living with another woman at the same time as continuing to lead what was in many ways for the children a 'normal family life' said,

> I'm still holding onto a bubble which burst a long time ago . . . I can't go on with this kind of abuse . . . in the West we are breaking down as families but in the East we go to such lengths of deception . . . twenty years ago we would have come to an arrangement, the woman does her thing, the man does, the woman cheat, the men know, the men cheat but they don't let their women know . . . but they stay together because the family is the ultimate and most important thing . . . and now that's not possible any more.

In four families in our group the nature of the relationship between a separating father and mother remained hazy over a number of years. The absence of explanation about what was going on led to the children developing a wish 'not to think' because to think might lead to asking questions and to ask questions or display open curiosity about discrepancies in the family pattern of daily life was perceived as too dangerous to a precarious stability. It could also lead to the child denying his own experience of what he witnessed, which over time led to bizarre behaviour in the child in other contexts as well as at home. In this situation a child may not only worry about the meaning or absence of explanation for himself, but also for a parent who he observes to be unhappy.

Betty described the way Simon, her son, was constantly watchful and followed her everywhere. He commented to her '"You know I sometimes worry that you haven't had a very nice life, mummy", and I have to reassure him'. However, her own reluctance to clarify the situation led to partial answers . . . 'I have to say to him, "look we are very fortunate, we've got a home and we've got enough money and we, you know, see daddy twice a week, even though you know he doesn't live with us any more" . . . I know that it upsets me and has upset him very deeply obviously, seeing me unhappy'.

Working with the Darnley family we saw each of the parents on their own, Simon on his own and then Philip and Betty together. In sharing their sorrow that their marriage had really ended, which included the fact that Philip was living with another woman, they were freed to talk more openly to Simon who in turn became able to express his anger more openly with his father. His father faced the fact 'that you hadn't really understood that I was living somewhere else until you'd come here', and told us he 'wished that Betty and I had been more forthright with him . . . because it would have helped him to accept it, and I think he's absolutely right. I think we both felt we were somehow making life easier for him by not involving him in it all, and I think we were making things more difficult for him.'

In the McGuire family, father's absence was a taboo subject because Mary, the boys' mother, was so angry about the fact that he had left her for another woman. The oldest son Tony was behaving towards his mother as though he wanted to punish her for having 'thrown dad out'. Mary's fear was that he might also begin to act like his father. Four sessions were held with the boys on their own and an equal number with Mary on her own as well as a number of sessions with Mary and the boys together. In the time on her own Mary was encouraged to draw up a list of aspects of the life with Sean, the boy's father that had been positive for her. She was asked to write down those that she was happy to share with the boys. She was asked if she was willing to sign the list and say she would stand by it, before she met with her sons to share her more positive memories.

Having established some good images of Sean in her own mind, Mary was more engaged in the idea of sharing these than she had been previously. She told the boys that he wasn't all bad, and reminded them of how he used to make her laugh 'he used to be good at telling jokes. Do you remember any of the jokes he used to tell?' The boys said they did and they shared some jokes together. She went on 'he was nice and all that if he wasn't drinking or taking drugs. He used to help with the housework from time to time . . . '. We explored the boys understanding of drugs and the effect they could have and Mary made a distinction between Sean himself and the effect of taking drugs on his behaviour. 'He changed from being nice and caring, he use to show me that he loved me, he use to buy me gifts and that. He changed from being nice and caring and helpful and loving ... Cos he was taking all these drugs.'

In a family session two months later, Tony volunteered to give his mother a certificate of good mothering telling her solemnly 'you are a good mum, you've brought up two boys who love you and you've done a good job'. His work at school had improved and he had moved to the top of his class. Our belief was that the open discussion of the good things that his father had contributed to family life early in the relationship between mum and dad allowed him to worry less about what kind of man he might become himself, as well as making it clearer why his mother might have chosen his father as a partner.

Family interviews

We have used family interviews with both parents present in the room with their children in three main ways:

To acknowledge sadness about the break-up of the parents' relationship and the dissolution of the former family life

This has taken place in the context of helping parents explain to their children that living arrangements are now going to change. Where possible this has been accompanied by looking at what may be good in the future, accepting that a marriage that was not working has now ended, and getting the parents to explain to the children that they will now have good relationships with each parent in the time to follow. In the extract that follows a couple are struggling with finding it hard to be clear with their sons what is going to happen.

The mother begins by asking her youngest son, 'don't you know about mummy and daddy? We said last week, when daddy was away, I explained everything, I said that daddy might move house very soon and we would stay in the house. You would stay with mummy and you would see daddy at the weekends and as much as you can. Didn't I say that?' Her son denies that he has heard anything about it and indicates that he does not wish to know. The father talks briskly about what information he has shared but becomes softer as he shows his struggle in deciding to leave. 'I talked to all of them about the difficulties that mummy and daddy had been having together and the fact that I was going to be living away sometime in the near future, and that I was going to be living away because we felt that it would be better to have less arguments and less tension than would be the case if we were living at home.'

The children show that they have different understandings of what is going on, the elder son taking a practical approach. 'A lot of people in Britain are getting divorced, so, if you don't get on together, I suppose, you live apart.' We point out 'it seems a little bit difficult for Dave [the youngest] to understand that mummy and daddy have reached a decision to not live together as a family any more. There seems to be a part missing...' and mother takes it up: 'I think what is missing, is that we should really have sat down, me and Henry [her husband] with the children and explained to them all, but I think because I have always had more...I've always spoken more and brought more courage.' Then Henry interrupts strongly, 'I don't want to move out of the house, because I don't want to move away from my children. I do want to move out because I'm not getting on with mummy and we seem to argue every time we talk to each other but I also want to stay in the house because I want to be with you boys...Now I think that overall, and I have discussed this with mummy, that it would be best if I moved out because I think reducing the tensions, reducing the disagreements would make everyone happy.'

To explain the arrangements for ongoing care

A second use of whole family interviews is to make sure that both parents explain to the children the arrangements that will be made for their ongoing care with each parent, as well as the exact nature of the contact that is planned in the long term with the parent with whom the children do not have residence. Such interviews are very focused and address what either parent or child have said in relation to controversial aspects of post-divorce living arrangements as they have understood these so far. We facilitate listening to each other's views which are likely to be different and sometimes oppositional. The aim is a negotiated and very concrete agreement concerning the children, in full acknowledgement of the emotionally laden nature of the small details of family arrangements and the powerful personal meanings they can hold.

An extension of interviews of this type may be when contact arrangements are varied, either because the child wishes to have

more time with one parent or because one of the parents themselves has been experiencing the arrangements as unfair and the
children have become caught in the middle of protracted arguments. As the project went on we saw more families who had
been separated for some years, but who were still in constant disagreement about arrangements . The arguments this led to had
affected their children's ability to think and their learning at
school. The nature of discussions often focused on very small
details, diaries in hand, timetabling the precise agreements that
the child knows have been made so that they are not held
responsible for any change in subsequent weeks or months. We
found the most positive framework for these negotiations was to
express our belief that each parent was genuinely trying to do
their best by what they believed the child's wishes to be, combined with an acknowledgement that there would have to be
compromise on both sides.

To deal with contact issues

A third main use of whole family interviews has been to sort out
affect-laden issues in relation to contact; issues that may be as
much to do with unresolved feeling between the adults as to do
with the welfare of the children. Some of these interviews have
taken place many years after the legal arrangements have been
made. Unlike an intact family, many of the points of view that
need to be expressed reflect key differences that have led the
parents to be unable to live together. For one of us to have
spent some individual time with each adult has been an essential
precursor to bringing parents together for such a meeting.
Individual meetings also enable the professional to predict
where potential flash points are likely to be. By providing a place
where the individual meanings invested by each parent in their
child is understood by us, we hope to create a safe base for each
adult, as well as the children. In this context children know they
do not have to do the job of 'managing' the disputes. We take
responsibility for redirecting the session into a more useful
frame, when arguments become inflamed or bogged down. In
our view the original intimate social system in which misunderstandings were developed, the original family, sometimes may need
to be present for the misunderstandings to be re-experienced,

deconstructed, given fresh meanings and associations and as a result changed.

In the extract that follows, two children aged seven and six are discussing their anxieties about seeing their father, who they think is drinking too heavily. The presence of their mother gives them confidence in addressing a problem that they have previously only discussed with the therapist:

Jimmy: Well sometimes he's nice and then sometimes he's horrible.

Jane: Yeah.

Jimmy: I think that the times when he is not nice is maybe some of it is because he is a bit angry because he has been drinking.

Jane: Yeah dad, drinking makes you angry.

Mr S: Well, the last time we were together I wasn't drinking at all, but you still thought I was a bit...

Jimmy: Dad, remember when you said that thing about mummy is trying to keep the wall around us? I don't think that is right, dad.

Mr S: Well, it's what I felt.

Jimmy: I think...

Mr S: It's what I felt.

Jimmy: At that moment.

Mr S: At that moment.

Jimmy: But you don't feel it now?

Mr S: Perhaps less so now because we are all here talking openly and your mummy is here and it feels OK.

Jane: I don't think exactly that mum wants to keep a wall round us...I think she wants us to see you but only if you are in a good mood and when you're not... [drinking] you'll be nice to us.

Mr S: Well Jane, let me explain to you, I've got a lot of things that which are worrying me at the moment.

Jane: Like what?

Mr S: Well, financial worries, big worries. Now, sometimes people are not all in the same mood independent of drinking. Grandpa sometimes is cross with you and speaks strongly to you at the dinner table about something. I mean he'll even get cross, sometimes people are feeling depressed. You can't expect...I don't think there is any such thing as a 'normal' mood. You get cross.

Jimmy: Yeah I know.

Mr S: Look at Jane, she gets cross and wacks you. I could say that's not a normal mood but its part of a range of emotions and feelings.

Jane: I think that when you're in a mood and we're not doing any-
           thing except things that we should be, you shouldn't be too
           cross.

Mr S: Like what?

Jane: Anyway I don't know, I can't think of something at the moment
           but instead of telling us off for the little things, I do agree tell us
           off, but at something big not something little.

It is not only through talking that such changes take place but
also through powerful feelings. As another father put it, 'in survey-
ing the battlefield over the memories of young love and the carn-
age of the years between', the witnessing and participation of the
therapists had been essential in moving from the trenches, or
'entrenchment', to fresh positions. He defined this as including
forgiveness and the ability to shake hands and plan for the future.
Such plans include agreements about action plans that parents
will try to stick with.

The interviews may overlap with the orientation of mediators,
although the route of referral and the work along the way is
qualitatively different. While mediation has developed as a separate profession alongside counselling and family therapy, the
work with families and children in the context of divorce has
many points of intersection which can be further developed in
future years. This is discussed further in Chapter 10.

The goals of the work

The goal of our intervention is to contribute to family members
becoming more secure in relation to managing their own lives
and their children's lives. As a part of this process we would hope
to help parents move from a reactive to a more reflective narrative. The notion of 'reflective self-function' in adults (Fonagy *et al.*,
1994), the ability to take into account the mental states of self and
others, has been found to have a predictive value for secure
attachment in children. While the context of adult attachment
research is very different from the kind of hectic clinical exchange
that family work after divorce sometimes involves, the implications of attachment research for us as professionals *intervening in
the current context of a child's life* is to use our different positions as

clinicians to enable a context for a more reflective mind to develop. For each of us this is an important indicator of what may be a worthwhile therapeutic aim. A milieu where reflection rather than angry reaction becomes a more normal mode in previously oppositional couples, or a milieu in which thinking about what is going on and speaking about it is an open part of life rather than taboo, may create significant differences in moderating discord and denial and the effects of these on children in years to come. The implications of this work for other professionals working with children and families are discussed in Chapter 10.

We have offered individual and couple space to the parents so that old stories can risk being told in new ways. New connections can also be added, 'I loved you passionately...and then there was war...', rather than the denial that there was ever any love or connection. The former meaning of family life can then be better held onto during the divorce process because former good experience is seen to have potential new meanings in the future. These meanings are particularly located in the children the 'joint product' of the marriage.

Summary

Goals of the work

- *Focus* A move from 'battleground' to cooperating around parenting as the primary task.
- *Opinion* A move from one oppositional view to the development of a number of views on how disputes around the children might be framed and thought about, and a number of solutions to practical problems to do with shared parenting put 'on the table'.
- *Affect* A shift in the affective view of one or both parents towards the efforts made by the other. A shift in understanding how the child might be experiencing some of the emotional aspects of the relationship transitions.
- *Attributions of intention* (a 'new narrative') The development of new descriptions, ideas and perceptions of meaning seen in both the other parents and/or the child(ren)'s behaviour shared in a family interview.

Key points

- By having the opportunity to give their unedited story, both adults and children are freed to develop a new perspective on what is happening.
- For children, sessions provide the opportunity for them to speak to someone outside the family who is skilled at listening, who is neutral and can elicit what is of concern to the child. In the process, the child's understanding of the many differences involved is clarified. Subsequently in family interviews the child's voice can be more clearly heard and the child absolved of the responsibility for holding all the differences together.

  The main effects of the work are:

- Helping the families to evolve a narrative, however slender, in which there is a positive story-line about the life of the family prior to the decision to separate.
- Freeing the children from personal blame.
- Dealing with anxiety and uncertainty about how to 'look after' a distressed parent, and absolving the child of that total responsibility but acknowledging that they do have a part to play.
- Emphasising that each parent continues to love the child, and that the child has a continuing relationship with each of them.
- Enlarging children's knowledge about an absent parent where a parent has broken off contact, helping the child/children to deal with pain and sadness ... trying to find a positive frame for understanding that behaviour.

Appendix: the practical framework for the family work

The families in the project were referred over a period of six years. The project was explained in the introductory letter to parents as both exploratory, as well as therapeutic. In acknowledging that divorce is a stressful experience for all involved it was framed as a stressful life event from which we wanted to learn the particular difficulties each family were having and the solutions they had found.

1. The referred child(ren) and the parent with whom they lived were invited together to describe the difficulties they were having in the context of the family transitions.
2. Following this, the parent who lived away from the family home was invited in to tell their story and express their concerns about the children.
3. Each parent and the children were offered one or more individual interviews, and a family interview was also arranged.

Adult interviews

Each individual's version of the story of the changes that had taken place in the family was actively elicited and explored within the context of each adult's own story of their upbringing. With the parents this was done through a semi-structured interview looking at changes in the family over time; and subsequently by listening to each persons narrative with its distinct features, highlights and sorrows. Some parents sought further work on their own childhoods, and some women sought much longer help in unravelling the long-term effects of violent marriages often contextualised by a former experience of growing up in a violent family.

Childrens interviews

The interviews with the children were semi-structured and included drawing and play material. With a small number of children a CAT (Childrens' Apperception Test) was used to look at the particular variations children brought to the same experience of parental separation. Examples of the children's responses are examined in Chapter 5. A fuller discussion of the use of projective techniques will be found in Chapter 10.

Family interview

A number of key groupings in the family were seen together, to look at the different ways the stories were told in the context of different relationships, and to explore the active relationships and the quality of communication between parents and children. These interviews followed the individual interviews. Where it was possible for the parents to sit in the same room they were seen together. These sessions were usually highly affect-laden and the therapists kept them task-focused on 'what needs to be done for the good of the children'. While we were explicitly not into 'mending' marriages, the reworking of aspects of old misunderstandings often became a vital component of the coparent couples interview.

At this stage it usually became possible to start to compare or comment on differences in the way the same series of events could be seen by each party, and by acknowledging the painful feelings that usually encompass divorce as a social experience more affective responses could be brought in if these had been missing. The common nature of parental difficulties was stressed, and the particular features of difficulty for each family were elicited as well as the strengths or positive things parents were contributing to children being openly discussed. The children's efforts to clarify and express their needs as well as their struggles towards adapting to change were always acknowledged.

5

THE CHILDREN'S PERSPECTIVE: ENABLING THE CHILD'S VOICE TO BE HEARD

Divorce and separation are a difficult transition and very often the parents find themselves at a loss about how to explain to the children how the break-up of the marriage has come about. The children will have many questions, and in the absence of an explanation will develop their own ideas about what happened. These unfortunately may include blaming themselves or seeing themselves as somehow contributing to the family break-up.

The parents for their part will have arrived at the point where, for whatever reason, separation seems the best option, or the only option, available to the family. Having made a decision which they believe is best for the children, it is difficult to accept or even acknowledge that the children will be upset about it. Most children would prefer the parents to stay together whatever the difficulties in the relationship: sometimes it is possible for them to verbalise this wish, but sometimes they are unable to put it into words.

Roy

Roy: Mummy I just want you both to stay together.
Mother: I know but...
Roy: Please...
Mother: You see, we were staying together darling.
Roy: I just want to know if you and dad will stay together.
Mother: Well, I've decided.

Roy: Yes or no!
Mother: I've decided not to stay together with dad, firstly dad and I
            don't get on together, and when we were staying together we
            weren't getting on and you were having a lot of problems.
Roy: But you were getting on!
Mother: We were not getting on, darling. One of the reasons we have
            decided, I have decided to leave dad is because I want to give
            you a chance to have a nice calm home where you can grow up .
            and you can learn things and you can have friends and at the
            same time you will be able to visit dad and make sure that you
            have fun with dad.

From the children's point of view, the divorce of their parents
may in some instances bring relief from a life of ongoing quarrelling and high levels of tension, and in some cases physical violence (see Chapter 6). On the other hand it can be experienced as a
tremendous loss, particularly in relation to the parent who leaves
the family home. In addition, there are many disruptions to the
children's daily lives which result from the reorganisation of the
family during and after the separation.

As described in Chapter 4, we begin our intervention with the
family or parts of it together, and then see the children and parents separately on their own. This provides an opportunity for
the children to express their thoughts and feelings and to be
helped to make sense of them, and also to make connections
between events and experiences so that gradually a more coherent story can evolve. As any professional working with children
will recognise, just seeing children on their own does not mean
that this context will set them free to speak about the most worrying aspects of their lives. It is important, therefore, to create a
safe context for the child to begin to share what initially might
appear a very confusing and fragmented story.

With some children it is possible to elicit the story through direct questions, but often it is helpful to make use of story-telling or
to use play materials and drawings in order to enable the children to
relate experiences at 'one-remove'. Our clinical experience suggests
that the narratives the children provide through stories, drawings
and play materials are closely related to their own experiences.

Roy, aged nine, was referred because he was presenting problems both at home and at school. He found it difficult to keep
friends, was rather unpopular with his teachers, was showing

aggressive behaviour in the playground and was difficult to manage at home. Roy's parents had decided to divorce following a prolonged period of quarrelling and violence between them, often witnessed by Roy. However, Roy could not accept the end of his parents' marriage despite it having been a violent and acrimonious relationship. The individual interview with Roy revealed that the parents had expressed very strong negative views of each other to him. Roy therefore felt compelled to denigrate each parent in the presence of the other. He talked of his mother being 'bonkers' as his father had been referring to her as 'mad'. Likewise, when he was with his mother he felt unable to talk about the positive aspects of his relationship with his father which he very much valued.

Roy's relational world was one of confusion and desertion. When he was shown the CAT (Children's Apperception Test) cards, which depict scenes involving different animals interacting in various contexts, his stories referred to orphanages, dead people and rocks. It was impossible for him to use the stimuli of animals interacting together to build up stories of positive and constructive relationships. He brought toy monsters to the session and talked about frightening stories he had read and watched at home.

Following the individual session, we asked his mother to join us in an attempt to help him listen to her explanation for the decision to separate. In the excerpt earlier in this chapter he was begging his mother to stay with his father and refusing to accept his mother's explanation for the end of the marital relationship. One of us suggested he listen to her:

ED: I want you to just listen to mummy because I know this is a big worry for you and you have reminded me that it is even a bigger worry than thinking about your friends. So I want you to be clear about what she says.

Roy did not have a coherent story of his parents' marital break-up. His continual exposure to conflict led to confusion and anger, and his reaction was to cling to the notion that his parents should stay together no matter what. In the early stages of the work he was preoccupied with defending himself from his 'enemies': 'I have a curse chain so I can curse anyone I want, my enemies at school'.

ED: Tell me about your enemies.

Roy: They keep blaming me for things I haven't even done. Like Thomas, he keeps saying I nicked his Super Nintendo.

ED: And when he blames you, does any one believe him or do they believe you.

Roy: No one ever tells him off.

ED: You've told me about your enemies, now tell me about your friends.

Roy: Lots, most of the school are my friends.

And later on in response to a card depicting a lion and a mouse:

Roy: The lion is sad, he has no friends, everyone thinks he is a prat.

ED: No friends?

Roy: No, they're all dead.

ED: How did they die?

Roy: They just did.

ED: And what happens to the lion?

Roy: He dies of sadness...

There was also a preoccupation with seemingly endless violence. Looking at a card where the father dog was holding the puppy on his lap he said 'Look, he's spanking the dog, the spanking just goes on for ever, the dad is like a machine, four million years later the bones are cracking, there is nothing left...'

Gradually, in the course of our work, Roy learned to make connections between feelings and experiences and to distinguish between reality and make-believe, and to hold together the positive and negative aspects of a relationship. He developed a more balanced view of both parents and was freer to hold in mind either parent's good aspects when he was with the other.

ED: Do you worry about one of your parents when you are with the other?

Roy: Not really, sometimes I think about my dad when I am at my mum's, she gets me for two days and that seems quite long and dad gets me for one...

ED: You know that they both very much want to be with you, don't you?

Roy: Yeah

At a follow up interview, he could make a distinction between past and present and talked about 'old' enemies (at his old school) and new friends at his new school: 'I have about ten friends and about three enemies...people tell stories about me, people who don't like me, and then they become my enemies.' Roy also reported progress at school: 'things are quite good at school, for the past seven days I've been trying and I haven't been sent out once.'

During the work with the family we tried to address the need for consistency of parenting in order to provide Roy with an environment which would enable him to function as a child rather than as a referee between two warring parents.

Working towards a coherent story

Maria, aged six, had come to the clinic because her mother was worried about the effect of the divorce on her and her older sister. Maria was sad and unhappy at school and was having nightmares, and her mother found it difficult to cope with her at home. Maria did not have a coherent explanation for the family breakup but she vividly remembered a violent scene which had resulted in furniture being thrown out on to the road and her mother being hurt. However, it was difficult for her to put this in the context of a deteriorating relationship between the parents. She saw this as an isolated incident which resulted in mother and the three children moving out. Maria had no memory of things being difficult. She had been unable to express her feelings to the parents. The following was elicited in an individual interview.

ED: Did anybody actually tell you what was going to happen?
Maria: No
ED: Did Mummy ever say she wasn't getting on with Daddy?
Maria: I don't know.
ED: You don't know. I think it is quite difficult to think about that time isn't it? That was a worrying time, an unhappy time. It's quite difficult to remember isn't it? Was there anybody you could tell your worries to at that time?
Maria: No.
ED: It feels as if you have a very clear picture in your mind about how things went wrong when the furniture was thrown in the

middle of the road, but it is difficult to remember what you knew at the time and what you had been told. Maybe you weren't told a lot...Was there a time when you wanted to tell your mum and dad what you wanted?

Maria: I wanted to tell them not to get divorced.

ED: You wanted them not to be divorced.

Maria: Yes, and to stay together.

ED: Were you ever able to tell them that?

Maria: No.

ED: Was it hard?

Maria: Yes.

ED: Did they ever ask you what you wanted?

Maria: No, well my daddy did but I didn't want to tell him.

Maria was afraid that her father would stop liking her if she expressed her true wishes. The violent incident she remembered as an isolated instance helped her preserve the fantasy that there was hope and all would be well again between her parents. When playing with the dolls in a session, Maria again showed her anxieties about violence: 'Mr. Crumb shooted her and she got one of those green bits and it makes her die'.

Developmental differences

As explained in Chapter 2, it is very important to bear in mind the developmental stage children are at in terms of the kind of discussion which is possible to have with them.

Pre-school stage

When the children are very little, it is important to use simple and clear language in a way that a young child will understand. The term divorce might not mean much to a three-year-old, but knowing that daddy will not live in the house any more will. At the age of three the child will want to have some explanation as to how this came about and at this stage of development children do look for cause–effect types of explanation. Just as they want to know where rain comes from, they will want to know why daddy is not going to live at home any more. It is important to provide a clear explanation which frees the child from feeling in any way responsible for the decision or able to make the parents reverse it. Parents sometimes find it difficult to provide such an explanation and may prefer to believe that it is not necessary to do so with young children. In some instances it may be the teacher at the play group or nursery who is the one who will notice confusion and bewilderment in the child as illustrated in Chapter 2.

For young children the fact that one parent has gone may generate fears that the other might go as well. These fears may give rise to clinging behaviour, waking up at night or wanting to go into the parent's bed, or even bed-wetting or having nightmares. Some of these symptoms may be temporary and will subside with reassurance, but if they persist it will be useful for parents to seek professional help. The role of the general practitioner and health visitor in helping families with young children through the divorce transition will be discussed in Chapter 9. The effects of divorce in the school context are examined in fuller detail in Chapter 8.

School-age children

By the age of five when children start school they are beginning to make sense of the world around them and, as explained in Chapter 2, the security of their relationships at home will have a direct bearing on their capacity to explore and experiment with new situations and new relationships. Children who have felt loved and accepted at home, who have been praised and shown affection, will find it easier to make new relationships as they will have a basic belief that they are likeable and loveable.

As children grow and develop, their level of understanding and curiosity also develops, as well as their sense of justice and morality. They may feel puzzled as to reasons for the separation, they may feel a sense of outrage, betrayal or unfairness on their own or one of their parent's behalf. In many cases they will have the opportunity to talk it through with one or both parents, but in others they will find themselves caught in a loyalty bind which might prevent them from asking questions, talking about the issues that worry them or expressing their feelings about them.

In the following example, Natalie, aged 10, was expressing her confusion about the different rules operating in each parent's house and one of us was trying to voice what is best for Natalie on her behalf:

Father: Do you know what the rules are in each house?
Natalie: No, because we've never really talked about that.
Father: I think one of the reasons we split up is because we had huge differences in parenting, so we can have the freedom to parent how we want in our own home . . .
ED: I think one of the things we've been struggling with is to try and find a way in which things can come together for Natalie. Obviously, there would be some differences as you two are very different people, but it would be helpful if there could be some areas where you could actually negotiate a common way. It would make Natalie's life easier.

Children of school age might express their worries or distress through a range of behaviours or even physical symptoms: they may become distracted in class, uninterested in school or what is going on around them, they may seem preoccupied or listless and, yet, there is no information, no clues as to what may be going on for them. Some children may begin to behave in a disruptive manner, or may become aggressive towards other children.

Adolescence

In the clinical context, when we see adolescents self-harming, abusing alcohol or drugs or dramatically failing at school, there is often a connection between the onset of the symptoms and the break-up of the family or events associated with it. Maybe there has been a change in contact circumstances, one of the parents remarrying, or there are new step-siblings to contend with (see Chapter 7). Some of these young people resort to extreme behaviours to show their distress in relation to what has happened in the family. Sometimes it is left to the teachers to pick up the pieces as illustrated in Chapter 8.

What the clinical experience shows

Loyalty dilemmas

When parents decide to live apart the children become acutely aware that they will hold information about both parents which will not necessarily be available to one or the other. Our experience with children coming to the clinic is that from quite an early age they show how they can get caught up in loyalty binds in order not to upset either parent. The following are some examples:

Paul, aged six, calls his own father by his first name in front of his younger half-sibling in order not to confuse him. 'If I call him daddy, Steve will get confused because he calls his dad [Paul's stepfather] daddy'.

Laura, aged 10, who usually has a number of social activities on a Friday after school, will say she doesn't really want to go to the party when dad wants her to come to him on a Friday in order not to upset him.

Rebecca, aged five, was quite anxious about going swimming with dad, but unable to say so to him. After some exploration in a session with her and her older brother, we were able to establish that she didn't really like going into the male changing rooms. Father was taking her with him because he was anxious about her going on her own to the female changing room. Her brother came up with the suggestion they should book a 'family' changing room. The children had to be helped to voice the concern to the father as, again, they did not want to upset him.

Parent watching

We have seen children become 'parent watchers' concerned about a parent's mood or the state of their physical health. Robert, aged nine, was finding it very difficult to concentrate at school and on occasions became very disruptive. His relationship with his mother was deteriorating as they got caught up in an escalating pattern of confrontation. During an interview with Robert on his own, it became clear that he was very worried about his mother's health. She had recently had an operation which had not been talked about at home, and in Robert's view, 'mum works too hard, so she is always tired and I am worried she is going to get sick again'.

ED: Who takes you to school in the morning?
Robert: My mum, sometimes, but when she can't drive, um ... when my mum can't drive because she had an operation, she gets a friend to take us.
ED: What kind of operation?
Robert: Uhm, something in her legs, somewhere, she had to go into hospital ...
ED: Did anybody explain what was going to happen to mum?

Robert: No, they just went.

ED: You must have been very worried.

Robert: A bit worried.

ED: When you were worried, Robert, who did you talk to about your worries?

Robert: No one

ED: So, probably all these worries keep buzzing in your head and that's why you can't concentrate at school. It might be easier if you had things explained to you. You must also be worried about what is going to happen to all of you if mummy and daddy decide not to live together any longer.

Robert: No, not really, they argue too much.

Giving up their own wishes

Jim had just transferred to secondary school when his parents separated. Mum wanted to move away and it was very difficult at the time to listen to Jim who desperately wanted to remain in his new school which he really liked. Jim was finding it difficult to voice his wishes, and it was necessary for one of us to speak on his behalf about the need for continuity in his education which we were then able to discuss during a family interview. The parents had not fully appreciated the strength of Jim's feelings, and even though mother was still determined to move it became possible to talk about the dilemma for the family and the consequences of the decision for each member of the family.

Monitoring what they say

Children can become guarded and over-careful about what they say to each parent about their time with the other. 'I think dad would be upset if I say I have a good time with Joe [mother's boyfriend], so I don't tell him when we go out with him', This was Pete's way of protecting his dad (and himself), but it took extra mental energy to monitor what he said and he started to lose concentration in class.

How to ask questions

It is important for the children to feel that they are not the only ones going through this process. Acknowledging that children often feel confused and uncertain at a time of change in their families is going to make the child feel less anxious, and it is important to find a time and place which makes the child feel safe talking about the home situation. For teachers, making a connection with whatever they have observed in the child's behaviour is a good way in: 'I've noticed you are easily distracted, not working as hard as before, is there anything going on for you?' Sometimes it is helpful to generalise or normalise the situation: 'Sometimes when children find it difficult to concentrate they are preoccupied with something that is happening at home . . . '

Our clinical experience shows that boys often feel very angry with their fathers for leaving them, but their anger gets expressed in a variety of ways. Being aggressive in the playground or getting into fights are some of the indicators to watch out for.

The need for a coherent story

We know from the Exeter study that only 1 in 16 of the children had been prepared for an impending separation or divorce by explanations from both parents (Cockett and Tripp, 1994). The children that we have seen frequently have a very fragmented version of what has happened, and it is often difficult for them to see the connection between the rows they may have witnessed or even the episodes of violence and the end result – one of the parents leaving the family home. The experience of the loss of the parent leaves them bewildered and angry, and even when parents think they have explained the situation, the children don't seem to be able to make much sense of it all. 'Why did dad have to leave?' 'Why couldn't they get it together?' 'If only my mum hadn't nagged him so much.' Or, 'I didn't know it was that bad', or 'I knew they were arguing because I heard them, but I never thought he'd leave.'

Sally's father had left when she was seven and there had been no contact for about two years. Sally was very confused and did not have a coherent story of what had happened. In the following excerpt of a session with her we are trying to develop an explanation by making connections between events leading to the separation, father's leaving and Sally's current worries.

ED: You say they separated because of money; if you were to tell me a story about their parting, their splitting up, what would you tell me? What actually happened between them?

Sally: 'Cos mum and dad had lots of fights, 'cos one day they had a fight and daddy just punched a glass and it broke, so we had to go across the road where my mum's friend lives . . .

ED: What glass?

Sally: We had a glass door, he was angry with mummy.

ED: Were there lots of fights? And, did you ever think that because of the fights they would split up? Did you imagine that – before it happened – did you think it would end up in divorce?

Sally: No, because mummy said it wouldn't happen.

ED: And what do you think now, do you think it's better this way? Or would you rather they were still together.

Sally: I would like another daddy [and later on in the interview] . . . I have a lot of fights with my mum . . .

ED: If you and mummy got on better together, would that help? Would life at school be happier?

Sally: A bit.

ED: Only a bit. Why is that?

Sally: 'Cos sometimes I get angry with my friend, I just get angry.

ED: And what do you think about when you get angry?

Sally: My dad, I think about him in my head, and then I get so angry with my friend and shout . . .

ED: So, you get angry with daddy in your head, thinking about him, and the anger goes to your friend but it doesn't really belong with your friend, it probably wants to go to daddy . . .

As mentioned in Chapter 2, it is crucial for children to be helped to make sense of changes in their family life. An explanation about what happened is the first step towards coming to terms with the transition.

Sam, aged eight, and his younger brother Ben were very confused about the fact that dad was not living at home any longer. On the one hand, the parents had played down the changes, 'dad has moved out because he has a lot of work to do'; on the other hand the children seemed to be seeing more of him, and at the same time they were noticing how often mum got upset and they saw her crying. Despite these very evident changes, no adequate explanation was provided for the boys. When they came to see us it was at the suggestion of the school who were concerned about Sam's disruptive behaviour and Ben's difficulties in concentrating. In the course of our work with the family it proved very difficult to openly address the changes. Father, whose new partner was now pregnant, had not even told the boys he was living with someone else, and his way of managing was never to take the children to his new place. Mother found it very difficult to help the children make the connection between her sadness and the end of her marriage, therefore it had not been possible for the children to express their sadness about their parents' separation or even make sense of it.

Children find it very difficult to give up the hope of an eventual reconciliation between the parents. Some of the children who come to us because they are experiencing difficulties at home or at school see a connection between their difficulties improving and the parents coming back together. As an eight-year-old put it, 'everything would be all right at school if they got back together'. However, it is not like that for some of the children we have seen. A boy who saw a clear connection between the father leaving and life being 'much calmer now' clearly was experiencing relief as the oldest child in a family where there had been a lot of violence prior to the separation. His sister, however, missed her father and felt sad about as she put it 'being forgotten by her father'.

Expression of feelings

An important aspect of our work is helping children to express their feelings, particularly those feelings of anger, disappointment and sadness about the situation. Parents may find it difficult to accept those negative feelings as they feel responsible for causing them, but gradually it becomes possible for the children to express them directly to their parents and for the parents to hear them. This process brings enormous relief to the children and enables the family to move on.

It is important not to pretend that the child doesn't know, doesn't understand, or that the worry will go away easily:

Nicky, aged six, was worried about who would look after her now that her father and new wife had a new baby. Nicky's father had been talking about how nice it would be for Nicky to change the baby's nappy and hold him, but had not been able to hear Nicky's anxieties about being 'forgotten', and losing her special relationship as father's only daughter. During a family session, it was possible to help Nicky's father explain to Nicky how he would take care of her: 'If we were all together, and Nicky and the baby were upset at the same time, Naomi [the baby's mother] would go and look after the baby and I would look after Nicky.'

How to help children find their voice

Verbalising feelings for them

Sometimes children need an adult to put their feelings into words. It is important to create a climate of trust in order for children to feel safe enough to let their parents know their feelings. This will increase the parents' understanding of their children's point of view. In an earlier example, Maria clearly was unable to let her father know how much she wanted her parents to stay together. Adults do not have to *do* what children say, but it is enormously helpful to the children to be *listened to* and therefore to be given permission to feel the way they feel.

In the following example, one of us is discussing with Robert how to share his worries with his parents:

ED: One of the things I would like to do is to help you share your worries with mummy and daddy when they come back. So that they know the things that worry you. Is that OK? I'll help you, I'll say it for you, is that all right?

Robert: Yes.

ED: Sometimes, for little boys and girls, it is difficult to say the things that worry them to their parents, because their main worry is not to worry their parents. I think that probably is quite a big worry for you. Do you worry about worrying your mum?

Robert: Yes, sometimes, a bit.

And when the parents join us:

ED: Robert has rather a lot of worries, but one of his main worries is not to be able to talk about them, so he keeps them in his head, and the worries keep him very busy and that is probably why he doesn't listen to the teacher at school ... and [to mother] Robert worries about your health, and your strength and whether you will be able to look after him ... another worry is, he knows you are going to split up, but he has no idea when this is going to happen, and that is a worry, he has some ideas about wanting to live with his dad. He would like to live here [Mother was thinking of moving abroad].

Enabling adults to listen

Sometimes it is difficult for parents to hear the child's point of view as it conflicts with their own interests or wishes. Following an interview with Emily, aged 11, we tried to convey to the parents how difficult Emily's position was:

ED: One of the things we've been talking about with Emily is how she has this big job, she has taken it upon herself to look after both of you. Which is quite difficult at her age. When Emily has a row with mum, she ends up looking after mum, she doesn't want to upset dad either. She is very keen to look after you both, because, I think she sees herself as responsible for keeping the peace between you ...

Father: You don't really have to look after us because we are not rowing. We are trying very hard not to.

Emily: I don't like to see mummy crying.

Sometimes children will be able to show their feelings or communicate them in a context outside the family. A story written at school or something said in class can give clues to a teacher about the child's experience. However, it is sometimes quite difficult to enable a parent to hear it. Again, a distinction has to be made between the adults making the decisions and their capacity to hear the child's distressed voice. A comment by a teacher in a non-judgemental way can be very helpful to a parent in these circumstances. In a secondary school, a form tutor noticed that Lisa, aged 15, had stopped doing PE, was wearing very baggy clothes and never seemed to be around at lunch time. Some of Lisa's friends had communicated their worry to the teacher. They thought she might not be eating properly. The form tutor who had a good relationship with Lisa was able to elicit that she was very unhappy since the arrival of her mother's new boyfriend. A meeting with the mother followed and the teacher was able to help the mother think about a sensitive way of handling her daughter's distress.

Helping the child to say it and the parents to listen
Once the parents are ready to listen, it becomes possible to help the child verbalise his or her own feelings. Children often find it helpful to be supported in saying things themselves rather than having an adult say it for them. But they have to feel confident that it will be safe to say it. That is, they need to be reassured that the parent will be strong enough to hear it, that they will not get cross, and above all that their feelings will be taken seriously even though the situation will not necessarily change.

Holly, aged 10, felt she had to protect her parents from any negative feelings in order not to upset them. After an individual interview in which we went over how she might communicate to her father her feelings about seeing him with his girlfriend, she was able to say: 'I would just be pretending to be happy saying, like if you asked me how my day was at school I would say fine, and I wouldn't tell you how upset I was.'

Adele, aged 10, has a very close relationship with her father and she and her younger brother see him regularly, though not often enough according to Adele. Father is now remarried and has a young child. When Adele visits, she feels she is expected to help with looking after the baby which leaves little time for the much-valued exclusive time with her dad. She feels she is losing out and is resentful but does not dare let her dad know in case he gets cross with her and stops seeing her. In discussion with the parents it became clear that the expectations of father's new wife were clearly that Adele would perform the role of 'older sister' to her stepbrother. The fact that she was only 10 and very much needed to feel that she was still 'daddy's special girl' had been overlooked. Discussion with the father uncovered his fear of upsetting his wife but helped to clarify Adele's needs. A compromise was found whereby father spends some special time with Adele and also with her brother during their weekend visits.

Adele has also been able to develop a relationship with her stepmother which she enjoys, sometimes they go shopping together leaving dad to look after the younger boys.

Modelling for ways of coping with loss
It is possible to help children understand and come to terms with their feelings of loss by modelling how to acknowledge loss and be sad about it. In a school where there was a tendency to minimise losses in order 'not to upset the children', it was possible to think with the teachers about different ways of managing loss and the effect on the children. In this particular school, when pets died the cage conveniently disappeared at half-term. Teachers conveniently left at the end of term so there was no need to say goodbye as everybody was going on holiday anyway. The belief held was that if the loss was minimised it would be easier to cope with. In the course of our work with the staff it became possible to think about ways in which children could be prepared for future losses such as teachers leaving, by talking about it, marking the event and allowing the children to express their feelings about it.

Talk about difficulties as well as advantages of having two homes
Children can be helped to adapt to their new situation if they are helped to understand the change and adapt to it. The idea of having two homes can feel daunting and exciting at the same time. Parents can be helped to think with the children about the arrangements in a way that makes it possible for them to feel they can contribute and be part of the process. One of the most important things for parents is to explain fully to the children what the change of circumstances will entail and *the implication for their daily lives*. For example, are they going to have to take the bus to school when they are with dad, who will pick them up, will they be able to have friends to stay, will they have to share with stepsiblings, will they have their own room? It is important to encourage parents to explain the practicalities in detail to the children and to make predictable arrangements. This will allow the children to feel more secure and less at the mercy of imposed change.

Sometimes it can be helpful to the children to rehearse with an adult how they might manage some of the less-familiar situations.

In a family session, Sue aged five and Ben aged seven had to be helped to convince their father that his shouting really frightened them, particularly when he drank too much. Asking the father to stand up next to the children was a concrete way to emphasise how much bigger and taller he was, and therefore how threatening it was for the children to hear him shout. We rehearsed, in the session, what the children had to say to their father in order for him to realise he was frightening them and stop.

Use of stories and play

Sometimes children find it easier to talk about 'one-removed' situations. We use toys (dolls and animals) to enable children to represent situations and relationships. We can then talk to them about the content and make connections with their experiences and their strengths in order for them to develop a different narrative about themselves. After listening to Philip's stories it was possible to point out to him how in the stories people were always able to find the resources to get out of difficult situations. He had described how a rabbit had managed to get out of his cage and find his brother and how those in a cave had survived the hazards of winter. It was useful to Philip to see the connection between the characters and his own resources (as he had created the stories). The use of stories and standardised stimuli like projective tests will be explored in Chapter 10.

Helping children to cope with family reordering

New partner in the home

One crucial feature in the restructuring of the family relationships as a result of separation or divorce is the often closer relationship between the children and the in-house parent. This closeness is threatened with the arrival of a new partner in the scene. It is common for the oldest child in the family to share with the resident parent in decisions and responsibilities, and this status is put in jeopardy when the parent repartners. The closeness is replaced by a new restructuring of the relationships, with the adults again forming a sub-system which leaves the oldest child in limbo. The research shows this transition is particularly difficult for girls who have developed close relationships with their single mothers (Brand, Clingempeel and Bowen-Woodward, 1988).

Contact with the nonresident parent

Most parents make tremendous efforts to make workable arrangements which pay off as it is much better for the children to be able to remain in contact with both parents. Sometimes, further work is needed to consolidate changes in arrangements and for the children to work towards accepting the end of their parents' marriage. This, of course, is not the end of the parent–child relationship, but it may need a new beginning. The children need to be clear about *when* and *how* they will see the out-of-house parent, and must be helped to feel free of guilt because they have a good time with either parent. We put a lot of work into helping family members differentiate between the different relationships. The husband–wife relationship may have ended, but the parent–child relationship has not.

When the nonresident parent repartners

Relationships with the out-of-house parent (usually the father) can also become strained when he repartners. Children have expressed concern about forming a relationship with their father's partner in case it upsets their mother. Parents who have a conflict-ridden style of relating, will find it difficult to discuss with each other the implications of their new relationships for the children. Again it will be very helpful to the children if the parents can agree on how to handle the transition and find a way of communicating the changes sensitively to the children. Children will have to get used not only to sharing their parent with another adult, but will have to adapt to new rules and patterns which will evolve with the new relationship (see Chapter 7).

It will be important to introduce the children gradually to the changes and for the parents to be willing to accept whatever mixed feelings the child might express. The implications of the new relationship will have to be discussed with the children so that they know what to expect. For example, are there stepsiblings who will sometimes be there? Will it mean sharing a room? What about authority? 'Why should dad's girlfriend have a say in when I go out or what time I come in', asked a 14-year-old boy whose relationship with his father had rapidly deteriorated since a girlfriend arrived on the scene.

Older children helping younger children/siblings

When children are together in a new and less-familiar situation, they can draw on the safety of their relationship and this must be encouraged and supported. Research evidence suggests that stressful life events such as separation may bring siblings together, although this effect is most clearly seen when children are of the same sex (Kier and Lewis, 1998).

Fiona was unsure about weekend visits to her father and stepmother, but felt better about it when reassured she would always go with her older brother, Adam. Adam, on the other hand, was very caught up with being loyal to mum and found it difficult to acknowledge any pleasure when they were with dad. Fiona was able to remind him that they enjoyed going fishing and playing outdoor games with dad. However, given that father and his partner sometimes abused alcohol, there wasn't a sense of safety for the children during their visits. During our work with this family it became possible to draw on the grandparents as a resource for the children. They were able to see their father in the safety of the grandparents' home and continue the relationship without feeling unsafe.

The complexity of the relationships children have to cope with as a result of separation, divorce and family reorganisation must not be underestimated, and every effort that can be made to help children understand and manage this complexity will be worthwhile.

It is important as professionals working with children of divorce to enable the children to talk to us in a climate of safety and trust. However, it is not very useful to assure them of confidentiality as this would defeat the purpose of helping the child's voice to be heard. If children understand that we are listening to them and taking their concerns seriously and it is our job to enable their parents to listen, they usually feel relieved that someone is voicing their feelings, wishes and fears, or helping them to find their own voice.

Summary

- Even young children need to be told in simple terms that their parents will not live together any longer.
- Children may show their anxieties about the separation through various emotional or behavioural symptoms. Sometimes these are temporary, but if they persist it is useful to seek professional help.
- Children who feel loved and accepted, who have been praised and shown affection, will find it easier to make new relationships as they believe they are likeable and lovable.
- Children can get caught up in loyalty binds in order not to upset their parents.
- Watching or worrying about their parents can affect children's capacity to concentrate and learn at school.

Children need:

- A coherent story about the separation.
- Acceptance of their feelings and help to express them.
- Parents to listen to their concerns.
- Talk about having two homes and relationships with stepparents and stepsiblings.
- Predictable and reliable arrangements for contact with the nonresident parent.

6

BEYOND RATIONAL CONTROL: ANGER, VIOLENCE AND MENTAL ILLNESS

Divorce is often the end result of extreme emotional tension, and as a process may take place in that context. Such states do not usually place children at risk, although recent analysis of cases seen by family-court welfare services within inner London suggest that violence may be present in up to 45 per cent of families presenting there (Jeffrys, 1998).

In this chapter we consider some of the more extreme feelings and behaviours shown by parents that may constitute risks for children both before and after a parental separation. Whereas the idea and the final experience of separation may bring about greater safety from misperception, mistreatment or violence for one or both of the adult parties concerned, the initiation of the process of separation can precipitate an increase in domestic violence. There may also be situations in which children are at increased risk in the home of one or other parent, and in particular in relation to contact visits with fathers where domestic violence has been a major factor in the mother's wish to divorce.

Many agencies, both statutory and voluntary, are currently involved in coordinating responses to violence in the home. In this chapter we limit our thinking about responses to violence in the context of divorce to the experiences we have worked with or consulted to in school or in general practice. Recent initiatives in the treatment of men who perpetrate violence on their partners show that groupwork with men which focuses on their taking responsibility for their own actions, in addition to individual work as required, can be a powerful way of changing violent attitudes and behaviours. This is accompanied by parallel work with their wives or partners (Blacklock, 1998). Coordinated approaches in which police and social-service child protection services work side by side have shown themselves highly effective in reducing violent incidents in the home (West Midland Police HQ Family Protection Unit, 1998; Fulham Community Safety Programme, 1998). In our own study, none of the women we saw had sought safety in refuges, those who had fled their homes with children going to relatives or friends. We are therefore writing about a violence that is still responded to within a context of family or close relations, rather than requiring a specific resource dedicated to the protection of women and children.

Risks within post-divorce homes

We would like to consider the risks to children in one of their two 'homes', settings in which they are supposed to feel secure. A child may be 'at risk' through a parent's inability to provide a developmentally appropriate context for them when they are visiting. Many mothers report with concern such issues as children's bedtimes being ignored, children watching inappropriate adult videos with their fathers, or children witnessing their fathers in states of drunkenness, or sexual intimacy with a woman who is not their mother. Secondly, a child may also be required to take on aspects of the role of 'partner' in relation to one of the parents. This might include putting a drunken father to bed, feeding a drug-addicted mother, or witnessing emotional breakdown in which they are expected to take a position as a comforter. Thirdly, in addition to not being 'looked after', a child may at times be seen by a parent in ways that were formerly directed at their marital partner, and therefore 'used' in psychological interpersonal games that they do not understand.

Where violence has been a part of the marital or couple relationship this can place children at additional risk. Ongoing disturbance expressed in violent behaviour, which may have been held in the relationship between the parents, has to be handled in different ways as a child now confronts each parent on their own. What may sometimes happen in this situation is that a child can become temporarily misperceived as another 'grown up' person by one parent, and 'annexed' to form the 'other parent' in the mental representation of either of his parents. Where an individual's own view of themselves as 'good' or 'capable' requires another person to be assigned the part of a 'bad' person who has to be punished or shaped correctively, a child can be put at risk of playing that part. Where a parent has 'resigned' from the part of the bad person as a result of divorce, the child may in the other parent's mind take up the understudy position. New communication skills, as well as safer ways of managing conflict, have to be developed between parent and child, since the child can no longer rely on another parent being present to defuse or distract from an escalating conflict.

A number of research studies have looked at violent patterns between men, women and children carried across several generations, and have considered the ways in which young children experience and incorporate positive and negative adult interactions into their own ways of behaving (Caspi and Elder, 1998). These studies use the concept of 'internal working models' (discussed in Chapter 2), which are defined as 'affectively laden mental representations of the self, other and of the relationship derived from interactional experience'. In relation to violence, held in the mind as one aspect of a 'working model of a relationship', children may take on board complex patterns and carry them forward into other contexts in their lives (Sroufe and Fleeson, 1988). In their study, children could frequently be seen repeating different aspects of the violent behaviour done to them, or which they had witnessed taking place between their parents, being able to play the role of both abused and abuser. In our study, the number of referred children and their siblings who had witnessed violence was relatively small (13 boys and 10 girls, of whom two were said to be too young to remember anything). The number who, in addition, were reported as experiencing violence themselves or who reported it was much smaller (five in all). However we found evidence of violent patterns repeating in the behaviour of all but one of the boys who had witnessed violence between their parents.

We do not yet know enough about what makes a difference to the experiences of children who have been exposed to similar violence in the home, but we believe that age, gender and position in the family each play a part. The fear of violence recurring in the boys' behaviour towards their mothers, for many years following the parental breakup, remained a key issue that mothers found problematic and exhausting. This concern only featured rarely in mothers' anxieties about girls in the same households.

How can children develop sufficient flexibility in their own ways of responding to violent behaviour by a parent, so that they are not trapped by it and are able to break an escalating spiral of violent behaviour directed towards them? Obviously there are many gradations of 'violent behaviour'. In half of the families we saw with problems arising from violent behaviour there had been a persistent and recurrent mode of a man operating a system of power and control over a woman and children. In each of these families the women fought back and, although terrorised at times, retained a capacity to think and act for their own and the children's protection. These families were divided between those who left home with the children and those who forced their partners to leave, using court injunctions where necessary. In such situations the way a woman behaves may affect the way a child defines violent behaviour as something that should be stopped, which they themselves have a right not to be exposed to. We cannot always assume that children do believe they have this right. In situations where violent or sexually inappropriate behaviour has been part of the child's experience over time, *a child may be very unclear about what they have a right to say no to*, and this may be one of the first important things someone from outside the family can contribute, a belief in the right to say 'no' to a parent. Whilst there has been wide acknowledgment of the need to teach children the right to say 'no' in relation to sexual abuse, it has been less a part of public awareness in relation to physical abuse, which more often is seen as within the domain of domestic privacy.

Emde (1988), in thinking about the relevance of research to clinical intervention, addressed the question of how individuals make meaning out of repeated events and the way in which experience that is lived through or witnessed may become transformed into represented relationships in children's minds. For example, children's choices as to how to respond to violence may become limited because they only witness certain repertoires of behaviour. It is crucial to broaden their opportunities for responding differently by considering the child's world outside the immediate family, and what models of behaviour are on offer there! How do patterns established in families connect in the child's everyday experience with other social systems with whom the family interact? Do these other systems offer the opportunity for more *flexible* development, for different thinking and behaviours to be learnt, or do they reinforce negative and violent experience already learnt in the family?

Processing experience

Let us consider here how a young child can process a violent experience witnessed between his mother and father, one which replicates a scene he has witnessed or overheard many times.

Pat's mother and father had been separated for two years and contact had been going well. Pat was doing very well in his first year at primary school, but following a big fight when his father came to collect him from the school gate when he was drunk, his mother, Clara, refused him contact with Pat until he could promise not to drink while looking after him. Far from drinking less, Pat's father, Mike, responded by coming to her flat when he was out of control, breaking her door down and then trying to beat her up. While she handled this frightening event very well, and was able to protect herself from him, the event reminded Pat of other occasions when fighting had taken place between them. He started to have terrible nightmares and was unable to concentrate in school; as well as showing aggressive behaviour in the playground which had not previously been noted by the school staff. In talking with him he was well able to give his own account of the events which had scared him, although his mother said he had never mentioned these before.

GGB: Do you remember the shouting and fighting? Perhaps you used to watch it sometimes or did you run away and hide? Where were you when they were fighting?
Pat: I was standing near the door.
GGB: Right, so you could run away?
Pat: Just watched so they couldn't get me.
GGB: When they got very angry, were you afraid they might hit out at you as well?
Pat: Yeah.

Clara: . . . It always use to be when his dad was drunk. And he use to be frightened as to what might happen.

GGB: Was your dad different when he was drunk?

Pat: Yes.

GGB: What was it about him that made you think, 'Oh dad's been drinking'?

Pat: . . . They were just rowing. [shows GGB a picture he has drawn of the fight]

GGB: It is a very, very good picture, tell me who is who so that I don't guess wrong.

Pat: That's dad and that's mum and that's me.

GGB: Standing by the door so you can get away. That is a very, very good picture. [Pointing to the drawing] And did dad use to grab mum sort of by the neck or just push her around?

Pat: Push her around.

Pat revealed his sense of powerlessness when his mother and father were shouting

GGB: What did you try and do when you tried to stop them?

Pat: I tried to shout but they couldn't listen.

GGB: Yes, it's a horrible feeling when you're trying to stop someone and they won't listen.

Pat: Yes.

GGB: Did that happen quite often, do you think?

Pat: Yes.

Clara: He's never mentioned it at home.

GGB: Children often do remember frightening things, you know, especially if it's happening to people they are fond of. [To Clara] And did that happen very often, are you able to remember?

Clara: Yeah, too often. It was every weekend and sometimes during the week.

It seemed that Pat, at age five, had been able to dream his terrors rather than talk about them. His mother had not thought of talking with him about his father's violence partly because the events he remembered were events from which mother had wished to protect him, and partly because of the hurt of remembering them herself. Many parents also fear that by talking about an event they will make it worse rather than better. Clara wanted things to change for both herself and for Pat and his father. We ended the first interview with the agreement that any time he had a dream he was to go straight to Clara, even if it meant waking her up, to tell her about it. Pat asked his mother, 'Even at midnight?' and she confirmed that he could. Two weeks later she asked to come on her own, saying that there had been no more nightmares or bed-wetting but there were things she herself wanted to discuss.

For Clara the powerful meaning of Pat's drawing lay in the way it repeated events from her own childhood. She too remembered just such fights when she was little, and her own sense of powerlessness, as she had hidden behind a sofa. Going through all the fears and meanings that she and Pat might read into such violent episodes was very important to her, as she wanted things to be better for Pat than they had been for her. Following her own mother's divorce from her father she had not continued a relationship with her father, which she bitterly regretted. Her wish was that Pat should be able to continue to see his father, following the separation, as she had not been able to see hers following her mother's. Her goal was to become strong enough to feel safe in allowing Pat's relationship with his father to continue in spite of the former marital violence. As we saw in Chapter 2, she was able to be clear with her son that the separation was not his fault; 'You're too little, darlin' it couldn't be your fault in no way'. She handled his father's recent attempted violence by taking out an injunction to prevent him coming to the house, and negotiating further contact between him and Pat outside the house until she felt safe. She also decided to tackle some of the ongoing violence in her family of origin, by taking charge of her brother who was currently terrorising her mother in her mother's house; blaming her and 'punishing' her for 'breaking up the family home' some 20 years before.

In thinking about Pat, one of Clara's worries applies to many children who have had similar experiences. At which points might Pat's view of the world as including violence as one of the 'usual' behaviours between a man and a woman become relatively fixed and potentially self-perpetuating? At what point in his own development might it be important to open up this topic with him to see if there were other models of dealing with anger and violence available in his own wider family? For example, if a child sees his father hitting his mother but has models of a different kind of relationship available from the behaviour of his grandfather to his grandmother, or his uncle to his aunt, he may well be less likely to have the idea that the relationships between men and women intrinsically contain hitting as part of argument in daily life. If, however, his grandfather hits his grandmother, and his uncle hits his aunt, as was the case in Pat's family, it is more likely that he will develop the idea that violence plays a natural part in the relationships between men and women, unless other family members recognise that they will have to do some work to help him think otherwise.

We do not know how many families are violent in this 'closed' way, although reports from Women's Aid suggest it is a much greater number than has been publicly acknowledged or described (Kelly, 1998). Many families have alternative social and friendship networks available to draw on, in order to develop other ways for children to witness or process behaviour between men and women. However, it is known that violence in families is often accompanied by a degree of social isolation, which has a number of self-reinforcing effects. This makes it important for all professionals who are aware that violence is going on in a particular family to consider the wider networks of which the children in these families are a part. As Gelles (1987) described, families where violence takes place are often characterised by a lack of participation in wider social relationships which can offer children alternative ways of relating and problem-solving. The role of school is obviously vital here, and increasingly schools are putting anti-bullying systems in place which give children a strong message that violent behaviour is unacceptable (Kidscape, 1998). In addition, services like Childline offer a child a neutral way of accessing information about help and resources available in a particular area, as well as being the first safe place for a child to feel they can talk about what is going on at home. Recent initiatives being developed include websites giving information on domestic violence and ways forward for children, and pocket-sized information cards with agency numbers on them to be distributed free to all children in school.

Maccoby, a child development researcher who has studied violent behaviour in families, has emphasised the importance of the overall style of family behaviour in any family in influencing the child (Maccoby, 1986). Most families develop or possess a range of ways of dealing with the provocations of everyday family life. However, it seems that in families who resort to violence when they begin to be angry or 'mad' at each other, certain conversations and ways of reacting dominate the overall pattern of relating, and other kinds of talking or thinking become marginalised. The development of one kind of angry exchange and violent language at the expense of others is especially likely to happen during periods of high conflict like those that may accompany acrimonious divorce. Two parents discussing how to share the arrangements for child-care, for example, may swiftly move from disagreement about the realities of a father playing an 'equal' part to wider disagreements about whose 'reality' is the 'truth', and then take the next step into defending their 'truth' against the hostility of the other parent.

Mother: I think if you're at work and you hear that someone's at home ill, you don't register it in the same way as if you're home with them. As their dad you've no idea what it's like to have an ill child.

Father: All right, all right.

Mother: You just hear about it after, you wouldn't necessarily remember it.

Father: Okay, so you're saying as a father I'm useless.

Mother: Don't say okay like that, I mean the truth is, you have never, you know, all the time they've been at school, how many times have you taken them to school, collected them from school? How many times ... go on answer me that. I can count on the fingers of one hand the times you've picked them up. And then you turn up with that woman ... And you claim you could look after them.

Father: I know when they have to be picked up, I can collect them and I know how to look after them when they're ill. Except you don't give me a chance, you're always slagging me off.

Mother: And you've never managed trying to work and look after children at the same time ... you have no idea what it's like as a man, you've no idea.

Father: Have you any idea what divorce is like, you tell me that then.

Mother: No.

Father: Exactly.

Mother: What does that have to do with it?

Father: New situations, new realities, you know, that's all it is. You have to face the fact that I'm going to do it too.

Mother: Well then, I suppose what I'm saying is that I don't want you to, you'd be no bloody good at it.

Father: Well now the knives are out, new realities will be created whatever you want. Stop pretending yours is the only truth.

Confronting parents with the need to develop new realities, focusing on common goals for the children as well as examining sequences of aggressive exchange in detail, can expand the emotional vocabulary of the family away from this kind of narrow and rigid reactivity which is typical of many relatively controlled discussions about how to share arrangements. Where violence is part of the modality of exchange, however, four things have to be taken into account in considering how effective direct working with the situation is likely to be:

1. Can violence be prevented and are there measures in place for the people involved to know who they can call on to stop what is happening, or to take charge of the children? Do the parents know how to stop it themselves in the new living situation they are in, without involving their children. These questions need to be asked even more precisely in situations where children will be finding themselves alone with a parent during a contact visit.

2. Will any former pattern of violent behaviour stop for long enough between sessions for any positive changes in ideas, feelings or behaviour developed in the course of the professional meeting to be acted on and implemented? Complicating factors like alcohol and drugs have to be taken into account in making the gravity of the unfamiliar lone parent/child situation into an important new reality for a parent who is unfamiliar with being on their own with their child.

3. How much has the modality of violence in the family become part of the *child's* way of expressing themselves, either at home or in a number of other contexts such as with friends, in public places like swimming baths, and in the school playground? Has the violence become a core part of the child's experience of himself, and carried into other contexts?

   Children sometimes act out violent ways reflecting a parent's way of behaving. In these cases, parents need to modify their own behaviour rather than punish the child. In our project, some fathers would talk vehemently about their sons being 'rough' with their friends, but would not link their own 'rough' behaviour to their sons until pushed to do so.

4. A fourth linked issue in relation to safety for children concerns mothers and sons over time, long after the divorce may be through. How much has the violence become part of the mothers' expectations of how a male, whether adult or child,

will behave towards her. In these circumstances any instance of angry behaviour in the child becomes connected in her mind with violent behaviour received from a former partner. We found this to be a particular problem for boys when living alone with their mother and we discuss this further below.

Risks for children

While some adult workers, particularly those primarily concerned with child protection, police work or the courts, may be highly attuned to possible risks for children, this is more difficult for workers for whom domestic violence is not commonplace. In considering how a child may be at risk, all of us need to be attentive to issues of adult power and the silencing effect of coercive systems of power-driven behaviour on women and children's voices. Work with women often many years after they have left a violent context, suggests that even though a woman may have accepted that violence itself is unacceptable, the effect of years of living in a system organised about the possibility of violent behaviour erupting has long-lasting effects on a sense of security and of self-esteem (Gorell Barnes, 1978, 1998; Gorell Barnes and Henesy, 1994).

The incidence of reported violence to children suggests that within the non-divorced family, violence is more likely to be an issue in relation to girls. However, it may be that in post-divorce family contexts, boys are equally or more at risk. A boy may become at risk when visiting a father on his own if he displays oppositional behaviour in a situation unmediated by his mother. His own confrontative behaviour may provoke retaliatory responses from his father where a mother is not there either to intervene or to moderate the degree of 'punishment' that is given. Research in the UK has shown that it is more likely that fathers will seek to continue contact with sons than daughters (Simpson, McCarthy and Walker, 1995), so that, this aspect of risk may be something to bear in mind for all concerned with divorce work with parents and children.

It is hard to think about violence without anxiety. In the remainder of this chapter we give a number of examples of families where our intervention over time has been successful in helping a parent create a safer context for their children. We suggest some of the key points that may empower colleagues in other work contexts to see themselves as a resource.

In the O'Rourke family, Sean had to learn to manage both his father's anger and his own impulse to respond with violence, as he moved between two parents with widely differing expectations following their separation. His father's violent tempers had been familiar for years, but these had intensified during the divorce process. Sean wanted to continue regular contact, but was frightened of the irrational way his father hit him and did not understand the 'cues' that meant he was in for one of father's 'corrective sessions'. He had formerly relied on his mother June to control these, but knew that now on contact visits he had to manage dad on his own.

Working with Mr O'Rourke, (Michael) and Sean together the details of what actually happened when Michael wished to 'correct' Sean were discussed in detail, breaking down the sequences and linking each behaviour to bodily feelings of hurt, upset and tears. Mr O'Rourke denied that anything really violent occurred, and described what he did as necessary correction. He was, however, prepared to have serious discussions about what *good* parenting involved, which included 'learning new ways of how to be a parent after divorce'. He accepted that children could only manage 'so much' of this and that activity, or time spent doing self-improvement tasks, and that planned parental home-teaching projects set by himself would have to be modified. Attempts to disentangle truth and reality in this situation, as with others involving ongoing denial, may be unproductive. A hypothetical 'as if' frame, placing children's education in a wider social debate, was more productive. 'If such things were expected of a child of nine years old by a parent, how could the parent address it?' From a position where he was invited to contribute towards the advice he might give to another hypothetical parent of a hypothetical child, Mr O'Rourke was able to think about 'appropriate discipline' in a different way. A series of more appropriate child–parent interactions evolved and, because he had worked them out himself (with the help of the therapist), he believed in them and was willing to let them take the place of his previous, highly-reactive behaviour. In addition it was discussed openly with father and son together that they needed to find other ways of handling moments when father 'lost it'. Ways in which Sean could remind his father of his age and his size were developed, recorded and re-discussed at later interviews.

A key feature in reducing violence involved encouraging Mr O'Rourke to express his loving and protective feelings towards his son. These were validated by the two of us, who as professional women showed that we did believe that as a man he could manage the job of parenting his son on his own. Mr O'Rourke's ongoing commitment to his son was a vital part of his life, and he welcomed brief focused and intermittent opportunities to discuss these in an explicit context of 'developing what is best for Sean'.

Other studies have noted how a good relationship with one parent may mediate the negative effects of the violence from another. Working with Sean's mother, therefore, was a vital part of providing an alternative context in which he could build up self-monitoring reserves and belief in his own abilities.

Three things helped June with her own self-esteem in addition to the cessation of violence in her own life. One was Sean's improved performance in school which followed a calmer homework setting to meet the school's expectations rather than his father's; secondly, Sean's improved relationship with her as a woman who was his mother, a relationship which had formerly been undermined by his father's abuse of his mother; and, thirdly, that her ex-husband, Sean's father, started to listen to her opinions about Sean's care more than he had done when they were living together. His own realisation that Sean was now doing better in school contributed to him being willing to lessen his own supervision of his child's learning and to cooperate more closely with his ex-wife.

Key features useful in reducing parental violence in a post-divorce household

- Identify the qualities the parent admires or enjoys in their child; 'pleasure' in child.
- Identify loving and protective features in parent.
- Help parent identify areas of their own competence with their child – be specific.
- Validate these competencies in specific ways: that is, ask a parent when you praise your child what changes/improvements do you see?
- Give professional approval to what you think is good and be very clear about what is not acceptable behaviour to children.
- Use educational models to help parents work out new tactics based on your professional knowledge of children.

- Ignore any historical or cultural claims to make violence respectable and replace it with 'modern thinking', that a parent can see derives from your professional position.

Children's bad behaviour as 'just like your father'

There may be many problems when a child has to move between two separate homes following a divorce, and either parent constantly sees his behaviour as something he learns in the context of the other parent's presence. What he does in the mother's home is a reminder of the behaviour of their former husband, what he does in the father's home a reminder of their former wife. However, there are also problems for boys when their violent fathers disappear from their lives. We have found that where a husband has been violent, even very small pieces of bad behaviour by a son may carry the stigma of being 'just like your father'. Whether or not the father is still active in the life of the son, he is still active in the mind of the mother; and many attributions may be made towards the behaviour of sons which can contribute to confirming violent behaviour, rather than freeing them to develop other ways of relating to their mothers around a range of issues. For seven of the families where the children involved were boys, aspects of their own behaviour were seen by their mothers as like their fathers.

One family that we worked with over four years showed these difficulties clearly. Mrs Ling, an Italian woman married to a Chinese man, had lived according to her husband's model 'the man's job is to provide the food, the woman's job is to make the nest' for many years without pointing out to him or herself the contradiction between his words and the reality of their lives. She was initially working long hours in order to support his studies, as well as looking after her first child Harry. As her husband gained promotion, Mrs Ling reduced her own working times as the family increased to include two more children; a girl Melina and a younger son John. Her husband regularly used violence as a way of legitimising his view of male supremacy. In discussing the effects of this over the years she described how she still carried a lot of the feelings inside her: 'I do think it's affected me with all the children . . . I'll give you an example from today...I went to see if there's enough water in the car...and Harry comes along, my big boy and he says [she puts on a fierce voice] "mum, why you put that on my seat, a magazine, you know", and he threw that on the floor of the car and I thought, "well, you mustn't do that"...that is important to me..."why don't you just put it on my seat", and I said "anybody else would have done that, put it on the floor, *why you act like him*". I've flipped like that before and I can feel myself getting very angry...'. However, at this point three years on from the divorce, Mrs Ling was able to make some distinctions between her former husband and her son. She added that on the way she had said to him, 'look I shouldn't really have said that, that you are like your dad...I'm sorry I said, you've got your good points like everybody else...you're not like that I said...you mustn't throw things...you should say "mum, just move it please"...and I wont flip like that...'. In thinking about herself she added 'You see...I've got this anger...I think it's just the pain...and everything that reminds me...it just comes up, I want to bash, I want to hide and I thought "no, no I cant do that to my kids anymore"'.

The situation with her younger son remained more problematic, not only because he often said violent things towards her but because he provoked in her the retaliatory behaviour that she used to show to her husband...'I say things sometimes...I say "don't do that I'm going to kill you", and he says I'm going to kill you...yes he says to me "you're my wife, I'm your husband"...he's my husband...your not my husband, I say to him, you're my son, do as you're told.'

For some children the violent behaviour learnt from parents is confined to the parental relationship itself. However, studies referred to earlier show how children may carry the violent patterns they have learned forward into other contexts in their lives, being able to play the role of both hitter and hit in contexts away from home (Sroufe and Fleeson, 1988). We found that this occurred in the school context for a number of the boys we saw.

A recent review of the effects of violence in intimate relationships on the children of those relationships indicates the strength of links between adult violence, child conduct disorders and violence carried forward by those same children into adult life (Moffitt and Caspi, 1998). Professionals need to attend to creating discontinuities in children's experience of violence even after parental separation. Much work may need to be done with the mothers of children who have themselves experienced violence to free them from the responses they have developed to cope with violent behaviours over time, so that these do not become further violent responses towards their children. In addition, education programmes in schools directed to learning to negotiate and mediate conflict in different ways has been found highly effective in projects both in Canada and the UK.

Major mental illness and irrational behaviour

We know from many research studies that the adjustment of parents following a separation or divorce has a significant impact on how the child adjusts. Major mental illness in a parent may involve acute or erratic and unpredictable behaviour of moderate to high intensity. These behaviours can become additional risk factors for a child if the family breaks up, as previous buffers against the stresses or effects of the illness are removed or altered, and the child becomes more directly exposed. Interactions with a parent may involve a quality of random experience that is hard to make sense of, and in some cases this can also include violence or inappropriately abusive behaviour towards them or their brothers and sisters. For example, a child setting off for school may be told they are cruel or neglectful in leaving a parent alone and that they should be staying at home to keep the parent company. They may be involved in parental preoccupations of a bizarre nature when they are trying to do their homework; or they might be called to deal with apparent or real suicidal behaviour that they feel inequipped to handle. Such behaviours are more likely to occur when the child is not perceived by the parent as a child, as a developmentally-dependent human being in the process of growth and change, but is seen more as a wished-for caretaker. Alternatively, again, they may be seen as an 'object' hostile to the ill person, against which certain kinds of personal and interpersonal phenomena of an irrational kind become directed. Living with an ill parent may be particularly difficult for a child if there is no other adult available to act as a safe base, or if there is no other adult who can be called into the household to take over if the going gets too rough.

It is important to emphasise that while a child may cope resiliently with a parent who remains ill over a long period, or chronically ill over a lifetime, the experience of caring has its own limitations and constraints. This is also the case for adult carers, but a child being both dependent and developing will need to have other opportunities provided for them outside the limitations of the illness context ... 'out to play'. Mentally-ill parents can become so self-preoccupied with their own illness that they are unable to think of the needs of a child for whom they are supposed to take responsibility.

For Caroline, for example, looking after her mother was second nature, since her father had decided that he could not live with her mother's long, complicated psychotic illness and had formed a second family early in Caroline's childhood. Caroline lived with, and was looked after, by her mother with the help of her mother's parents and a powerful Christian ministry in her neighbourhood. It was often Caroline who helped to plan her mother's day, and provided companionship after school and increasingly during school hours. She herself became the object of her mother's preoccupations, and was constantly presenting for a doctor's certificate with some new and hard to diagnose illness, which her mother insisted only her own sensitivity was open to recognising. She was increasingly withdrawn from contact visits from her father, because of the health hazards that her mother hypothesised lurked in the second home he had formed, hairs and germs from pets and ailments from younger children. Caroline had to manage the tension between her mother's beliefs and her own awareness of how much fun she might be missing out on in her peer-based existence at school. A voice in her head sometimes told her 'I know I'm the real mother round here'. However, to say openly that she wanted to go to school and that she liked seeing her father and her half-sisters was seen as too disloyal by her mother, and was a subject that was forbidden at home.

What can help a child to 'be all right' in spite of much that appears 'all wrong'? As professionals we need to learn more about the varieties of reliable intimate adults on which families can draw: grandmothers, aunts, elder sisters, grandfathers, uncles and older brothers; some cohabitees and long-term friends, and also paid help *in* the family, carers who provide enough support for a parent to manage who would not otherwise do so. An understanding of the many small episodes of relationship with the ill parent and with intimate others who are well, which maintain the child's own positive self-image, are essential. Promoting aspects of home life that contribute to a child's resilience need balancing with regular interactions with a reliable adult outside the home who the child can talk to as well as best friends who provide another dimension to living (Rutter, 1966; Gorell Barnes et al., 1998; Rutter, 1999).

Searching for reliable others can sometimes fail, and it is also important to know when family and friends cannot provide a safe milieu.

Edie looked after her mother, Emma, more than her mother looked after her, following her mother's divorce from her father when she was six years old. This pattern was associated with Emma's long dependence on drugs since before the divorce. Emma's mind was becoming more confused and irrational, following the development of the Aids virus. On some days she would expect Edie to behave like an eight-year-old and go to school on time; on others she kept her at home to work for her mum and to make tea for all the crowd who came into the flat; which was acting as a drugs base for a number of users. Edie liked doing this job and saw it as an important responsibility, but felt threatened by some of the bizarre behaviour she saw there, which often included her mother having sex with different boyfriends. Edie only went to school on the days when Emma was well enough but she often felt that she ought to hang around 'to keep an eye on her because I don't like the people who come to our house and I don't like them doing my job'.

Emma's awareness of her own frailty became the overriding concern for her as her health deteriorated, and practical discussion about Edie's future increased. Each of Emma's known relatives, with whom she had fallen out over her use of narcotics was contacted, and Emma once again became connected to her grandmother and to an uncle and aunt. None of them were willing to have Edie live with them, or else were not considered fit by Emma, who then had the idea of Edie's father being brought back into the story of her life.

At an earlier stage in Edie's life they both had good evidence that Edie had been sexually abused on a contact visit. However, Edie herself was excited by the idea of repossessing her father, but while on a visit to him reported to me that she thought he had had an erection when playing with her, and this had made her feel unsafe. Her conviction about this was sufficiently strong for the decision to have her placed away from her family to be taken. Edie's favourite story was Roald Dahl's *Matilda*, 'You know how most grown-ups treat children as wonderfully clever even when they are stupid, well it's the other way round, this is the strange thing. Matilda is so powerful that she can knock things over just with her eyes that's because she's got so much brain power that she not using it . . . '.

Many young children, prematurely exposed to caretaking their parents, develop varieties of belief, similar to this one, about their own hidden powers, which can last well into adult life. With young boys this has often been expressed to us through the assertion that they are now 'the man in the house'. What is disconcerting for them is when their mothers appear to behave as though this is indeed true, and place responsibilities on them that they are not emotionally equipped to meet. In our project this belief in their own powers was expressed by many children. Expressions of power, alongside feelings of powerlessness at what they could not achieve were amplified where a mother was clinically and recurrently depressed.

Paolo, aged 6, had taken charge of his mother Isobel following his parents' separation. He witnessed violence between them and became highly sensitive to Isobel's condition as relationships deteriorated. He took his job very seriously keeping a close eye on all her activities and friendships in a way that caused concern to the family doctor who referred the family. In the room with his mother, his sister and me, he put his feet on the table and, wagging his finger at his mother, said 'I'm the man in the house now, you have to do as I say'. Isobel initially felt too low to disagree with him, but her morale improved following her own accommodation in safe premises being arranged. Introducing Isobel's own mother into the household for long weekends created a shift in the arrangements, in which Isobel herself regained enough of her own self-confidence to thank Paolo for taking care of her, but demonstrating that she had the resources to manage the home as a woman-led household in which he had a valued but not a primary role to play.

Signs to look out for on behalf of a child living alone with a parent suffering from poor mental health following a divorce

- Has the divorce changed the caregiving arrangements for the adult in ways that mean the child has to take on inappropriate responsibility?
- Have the changes placed the child at risk in physical or emotional or developmental ways?
- Does the child have enough opportunities for their own learning and play?
- Are there reliable relatives or friends who can be involved in supporting the family as a whole?
- Is there someone reliable outside the family who the child can talk to on a regular basis?

Current thinking between the three departments concerned with children's welfare in relation to violence and divorce, the Lord Chancellor's office, the Home Office and the Department of Health, suggest that an integrated representation service which includes all aspects of court services for children, will work towards closing current loopholes around women, children and safety in the context of contact visits in both the legal system and the contact system. It is hoped that supervision orders may have conditions attached, such as direction to treatment programmes, which will be a condition of contact. However, treatment programmes will have to be increased in order for such provision to make a difference since very few that work currently exist (Kelly, 1998). In addition, a range of conditions explicitly articulated around conditions of contact may add to the safety of both children and their mothers It is further hoped that the power currently vested in the courts for punishing breaches in injunctions will be increased.

Contact centres

Contact centres currently see their primary focus as providing a neutral base where fathers and at times other relatives may see their children. Contact centres are rapidly becoming the focus for a potential provision of a range of services designed to improve the quality of parenting between fathers and children (Simpson, 1994). The debate as to how this will happen is still in progress (Halliday, 1998). Currently contact centres do provide a place where children can be seen in safety although the constraints experienced by many fathers seeing their children under restricted or artificial conditions may sometimes work against their purpose of facilitating parent–child closeness and positive interaction (Bratley, 1995).

Summary

Violence, safety issues and children in post-divorce situations

- Are there measures in place for the child (in their own home as well as on a contact visit) to know who they can call on if they get scared or hurt?
- Is there evidence that complicating factors like alcohol and drugs may have to be taken into account in thinking about safety for a child in their own home or on a contact visit? In relation to contact with father, can a person other than a former wife be involved in assessing the unfamiliar lone parent/child situation, and make safety issues into an important new reality for a father who is unfamiliar with being on his own with their child. Are there friends he can call on if he feels the situation is getting out of control?
- How much has violence in the family-style become part of the child's way of expressing himself? If it has become a core part of the child's experience of himself, violent behaviour from a parent may provoke retaliatory behaviour from the child. This can make a lone parent situation more dangerous, particularly in an unfamiliar contact situation. It may be safer to involve a third party such as a relative or friend as the basis for visits or to stand alongside the parent who may be provoked into loss of control. Fathers themselves suggest the use of contact centres may be helpful if they are staffed by volunteers willing to promote the parental care of the child. (Gorell Barnes and Bratley, 2000)

- Following the ending of a violent partnership, mothers may need help in remembering to distinguish any rough behaviour shown by their sons from that shown by a former partner. Helping adults remember they are parents to their children by whatever means counteracts confusion in which children can become 'to blame' for former adult violence.
- Violence not only creates fear, but also lowers self-esteem. Women and children may need long term help in rebuilding their self-confidence in many social areas of their lives.

7

FAMILY REORDERING: NEW HOUSEHOLDS AND NEW PATTERNS OF PARENTING

In this chapter we consider some of the ways in which reordered families interrelate both practically and emotionally with the families that have preceded them and continue to coexist in different forms alongside them. Reordered families usually bring previous baggage with them, losses of former close relationships, hurt, jealousy and disappointment, many of the stressful effects of transitions still present in current lives. These stresses need to be taken into account by parents in planning the management of reorganised family life, and time needs to be set aside for talking about the hopes and plans for the future. Thought also needs to be given to the difficulty many children have in coming to terms with living in close proximity with strange adults, an issue that often escapes attention at a time of complex family change.

A formal 'stepfamily' is created when two adults decide to form a household in which one or both brings a child from a previous relationship, and the new partner is thought of as becoming an important adult and parent figure to their partner's child (National Stepfamily Association, 1991). However, many households come together in ways that are less defined. The relationship between the new adult partner and the children may also be unclear; children may be full-time or part-time members in these new households, and as they move between the households created by each parent and their subsequent relationships they will be accommodating to more than one family style and set of expectations held by the adults involved. In most instances these expectations will not have been openly defined between the adults. Adults will themselves be struggling with creating rules for living together with newly-met children which generally evolve as the interactions between them develop over time. Parent–child bonds often intensify during family break-up, and coping with the pressures this can create for new adult relationships is part of the struggle to create new family rules and patterns. In addition there are the pressures of managing the boundary of contact between the children and the parent who is not part of the second-family household.

Since second partners, whether formally stepparents or not, may be additional rather than replacement parent or adult figures in the child's life, the shared division of same-sex parenting roles between at least two people, mother and stepmother, father and stepfather that arises from divorce and new cohabitation, is one of the particular adaptations children usually have to manage. Children will have at least three, sometimes four, and in families that have reordered more than once, five or six 'parent' figures, carrying out different aspects of nurture, discipline and education. Philosophies between households may be coherent or widely divergent. Unlike cooperative kinship structures in cultures where these have developed to facilitate the rearing of children over time, these post-divorce kinship structures may not be working in harmony and may well be adversarial and in competition for a child's loyalty and attachment.

In this chapter we consider some of the tenuous beginnings that characterise many second families, and outline some of the factors we have noted that seem to make the ambiguities of relationship more difficult or more manageable for the children.

The focus on shared parental responsibility embodied in the Children Act 1989, has a potential influence on newly-forming family boundaries in many ways. In making clearly visible the formal social belief that a parent is for life, it challenges many of the emotionally preferred ways of forgetting old relationships and constructing new family lives that many parents choose. The younger the children at the age of separation, the more logical it often seems to a mother that the man with whom she subsequently lives is seen as their father, rather than the man whose genes they carry. The Newcastle Study (Simpson, McCarthy and Walker,

1995) has shown that in the context of previous and current acrimony and violence, many women wish contact with their former spouse to cease. Where a parent wishes to continue their involvement with their child following a conflict-ridden first marriage, hostile patterns of interaction between former partners may not cease with divorce. If a former partner is actively disrupting current stepfamily life – for example telephoning every evening and insisting on talking to their child during a family meal; or behaving erratically in relation to contact, thus creating disappointment in the child and messed up arrangements for the family as a whole – the negotiations of daily stepfamily living involve an active external third adult who is often not well-disposed to new family arrangements. Where each adult in the stepfamily has children from a previous relationship, such interactions and mutual provocation in relation to a former partner, still a current presence, may well be doubled. In managing these tensions, which are more likely to characterise the early days of reordered family lives in second partnerships, we found that both men and women use up large amounts of energy to keep some sort of balance between their own needs for an emotional or sexual life, and their children's needs, sometimes preferring to keep a partnership hidden rather than bring it openly into the domain of family living.

The Children Act 1989 emphasises that wider family links matter, with particular reference to grandparents. In spite of this, popular discussion of stepfamily life and its management rarely acknowledges the significance of the wider family and the importance of the ongoing roles extended family members can play in the development of children. There are also important influences for good and for bad that grandparents can have on their own child – the parent who is going through divorce and new emotional explorations. In our study we found that just under half of the mothers and fathers involved their parents on a more regular basis in their own and their children's lives following the original separation from their partners, creating a more connected support structure for themselves as well as for their child's regular weekly world. For some, extended family members offered child-care help, whereas others had troubled relations with grandparents and, in some cases, had cut off frequent contact. In such circumstances grandparents only tended to be seen for annual holidays or festivals.

In general, grandparents did not actively create trouble when their children declared a new relationship. Only in three families did parents report that a grandparent had commented critically on subsequent relationships they had developed. Two of the three families were women who 'came out' in lesbian relationships, and the father's parents expressed their hostility to this. In the third family the grandparents had a history of feuding which pre-dated the separation.

Dealing with a parent living with a new partner

Let us contrast a girl and a boy of the same age both confronting this common situation, their mother planning to live with a new partner who is not their parent after a period of living on her own with them. Each is reacting violently in different ways. The girl's verbal violence is an open expression of her own fear of losing her relationship with her mother. The boy's behaviour, while involving similar fears, involves more open acting-out of hostility to the incoming partner, and is shown in ways that are more physical and less verbal.

Dana, aged 11, rang to say that a crisis was threatening her family. When offered a time to meet she revealed that she did not like the fact that her mother, after nine years of living without a partner, had now found a man she loved deeply and with whom she was planning to set up home. Dana's sense of panic and fury at the idea of another person entering her mother's emotional world was expressed by her as a fear of being 'shut away from her mother'. As the interaction between mother and daughter developed in the room, it could be seen how important to her was her role in looking after the mother who cared for her and her little brother for nine years. 'I've always been grown up. I had to grow up quickly because daddy left . . . I'm used to being responsible'. She added that in her life nothing was as important as 'looking after Damian and Mum'. 'You've always needed me, and now you don't need me and I still need you'. She showed her anxiety at becoming redundant by saying, 'She's always looked after herself and Damian, but in a way I've sort of looked after her too'. Catching onto the power of this important job in the girl's sense of herself and her own identity the therapist said, 'And it's very sad to think of giving that job up isn't it?' She replied, 'It's because I've been so used to it, it's me, I'm so used to it ... and then this man comes along and says "Well, I'll take over that job, thank you'''.

Boys may be just as closely connected to their mothers as girls, in families where they have been encouraged to be so, or in situations where they have had to 'look after' a parent who showed vulnerability to a point of emotional collapse, drinking too much, drug addiction or more severe mental illness. They may be just as anxious about these connections being severed. However, it is likely that a display of watchful or caregiving behaviour will be tolerated less well by an incoming stepfather then will the similar behaviour of girls. It may be accurately recognised as trying to keep the new adult more distanced from the parent than is the child. A boy may be more directly responded to aggressively, and as a rival, by a new male partner than will a girl.

Joanne, her new partner Harry and her son Dean, aged five, came following a crisis-line call initiated by Harry who feared the violence of his own responses to Dean's 'possessive' behaviour of Joanne. 'He will not leave you alone, he follows you around like a little dog ... he pulls and pulls at your arm until its sore, and its Mum, Mum, Mum'. Joanne had previously been left by her husband Joel when Dean was eighteen months old, and had subsequently been in hospital three times for overdosing. Dean's concern thus had at least two levels of meaning, concern over how his mother would fare with a new man in her life, as well as for himself. The advent of a new man raised important questions for him. Would it mean that he was displaced? Was there only room in the family for one man at a time, as his father's disappearance following his own birth seemed to suggest? Was it a choice for mother between Harry and himself?

Dave, aged 10, was furious to hear about his mother's plans to remarry because the decision offered further proof that his mother was not going to return to his father (although they had been living apart for over three years). He had attacked his mother on three occasions, and had also hit his father's girlfriend in the face. 'She pisses me off ... I just found out that he was having an affair with her and I don't know if he would have told me or not'. The questions of where primary loyalty and 'proper' paths of communication lay in his family – between adults, or between parent and child – was for him, as for many children living with a parent on their own, a very important question. However, in discussion, Dave was also able to note some differences in his mother's relationship with her new partner which he found reassuring, 'You and dad were always quarreling, you and Jim haven't had a single row'. His preoccupation over whether his father and mother could stay friends in spite of each living with another person was a key issue in his own security.

In a more unresolvable conflict of loyalties, Sergio found that he could not manage the anger with which his father attacked his mother's second marriage and still stay friendly with his mother. Whereas his father, Alessandro, had himself had a number of passionate affairs which had each ended with violence, the ending of the third one resulted in him turning bitterly back on his ex-wife blaming her for the original breakdown of the marriage. A constant tirade of violent phone calls and recurrent abuse of Sergio for choosing to live with his mother led to him leaving his mother and stepfather to try and make his father's life happier. Once he was living with his father it became increasingly difficult for him to see his mother at all, and increasingly he sided with his father against the woman who had 'betrayed' both of them.

When a woman forms a second relationship with another woman, a parent may wonder whether negative behaviour in the children suggests that they are reacting to the lesbian relationship and are showing 'homophobic' attitudes. It is often the case, however, that the anger the children are showing relates more to their parent forming a new adult relationship which they perceive as being disloyal to their father, in the same way as they might perceive a second heterosexual relationship. They may also bring anxieties with them from their father or their grandparents about the effects that growing up in a lesbian household could have on their own gendered development. Recent British research on children growing up in lesbian families, including stepfamilies, has provided useful information showing positive outcomes for children, in spite of their anxieties about prejudice encountered in school. It has been valuable to be able to share this knowledge as part of the wider discussion with both fathers and mothers (Tasker and Golumbuk, 1997).

We have come across situations where negative attitudes towards men held in an otherwise all-female household have proved too difficult for an adolescent boy to manage:

A 14-year-old, Seth, living with two sisters and his mother, Jane, and her partner, Rose, found that being at the receiving end of too many remarks aimed at men's negative attributes made him feel too alienated within his own home. Jane and Eli, Seth's father, had separated bitterly and with a lot of violence, and Seth found himself constantly dealing with remarks about male aggression; as he saw it whenever he stood up for himself in a 'house full of women'. He became progressively more marginalised from his family and more connected to a peer group who used drugs on a regular basis. His mother finally asked his father to take over his care when the school excluded him. Eli was dismayed at having to take over a son with whom he had not lived for four years, and had to rearrange his work-life and premises to accommodate his son in the two-room flat in which he lived. He also had to rearrange his free-wheeling sexual partnerships to take account of his son's presence in the home. Seth initially found the transition to an all-male household both difficult and surprising, because his father demanded far more of him in the household and in relation to his schoolwork than his mother had done. The use of his aunt's house, where two female cousins also lived, provided an alternative weekend base which helped him accommodate the new gender balance in his own adolescence.

Contact with 'the other parent': fathers living outside the children's home

The fact that a father does not live with his children does not mean that he does not play an active part in their lives, or in his children's minds. For some children, who find it hard to assimilate the fact of a father's daily absence from their lives, this absence can become a more powerful presence than when he lived with the family. When the importance of an ongoing connection with a father is not recognised in reordered families, this may create a greater rift between a mother's second partner and her children than in families where the importance of the children's own father is openly acknowledged and taken into account.

Simpson, McCarthy and Walker (1995), in their Newcastle study of fathers following divorce, report the numerous practical ways that fathers feel they can continue to offer support helping with homework, escorting to and from school, attending parents' evenings and offering an alternative base for the child. Furstenberg (1988), following up young people after divorce over many years, found that it was important for fathers to maintain contact throughout the children's lives even if they only saw their children very infrequently, and that this correlated with higher self-esteem in young people.

We found that parental relationships before, during and after divorce did not remain constant. Once the process of physical separation had taken place, and in the context of our own involvement with the family, many parents moved from an oppositional stance to one where cooperation over the children was possible. This may highlight the importance of having services available for parents at times of high-conflict separation and reordering, since research into families where no professional presence exists has suggested that patterns of conflict and interparental opposition may not change. Our time spent with families demonstrates the value of a neutral space to think about arrangements for the children, and to review how they were working.

For many fathers, separation involved a relationship with another woman which had been previously hidden. Where she was part of the children's contact experience, fathers often tried to define the relationship in a way that did not depict the woman as a rival to the children's mothers. This was more successful with younger children (under five), but was less so with children over seven who were likely to be more persistent in asking questions about the nuances of the relationship. Whereas some children openly objected to their fathers involvement with girlfriends, others only showed their upset where they associated a new relationship with less fatherly behaviour during their visits (for example father and girlfriend watching adult videos, kissing and cuddling while watching television, or more flagrantly walking around with no clothes on or being seen drinking together in ways that led to father's behaviour changing to the unfamiliar. Some children accepted the existence of a girlfriend relationship, but became angry at evidence of this becoming a marriage or formalised cohabitation (for example buying a flat together, or buying a dog). This was perceived as a much more direct threat to their own mothers, and a more explicit statement of the end of the previous marriage and family. As one mother put it in relation to her husband from whom she was not yet divorced, 'first the flat, then the dog, next a baby'. It is a common fear for women whose husbands have left, that a new relationship will lead to a father diminishing his involvement with his children, and research from the USA has shown that new family responsibilities may take time and attention away from earlier family relationships (Seltzer and Brandreth, 1994).

Other research (Gorell Barnes *et al.*, 1998) has indicated how complex the factors that keep fathers connected with, or more distant from, their children can be. A mother's wish to integrate her new partner into the new second 'family', for example, plays an important part in the way she encourages or discourages visits from the children's father. Walker (1997), in a small study of fathers' own accounts of how they maintain a balance between fathering and stepfathering, describes the multiplicity of ways in which events can interact to discourage fathers from maintaining contact with their own children. The attitude of their second partner to the commitment to the task of continuing involved fathering is crucial. Gorell Barnes and Bratley (1999), in a current study of fathering post-divorce which is focusing on what helps men to maintain the parenting relationship, examine (1) extended family factors, (2) the role of male peers acting as a support to father, and (3) the behaviour of children themselves in helping fathers to maintain their belief that they have a role to play in their lives.

When a father who no longer lives with the children places a huge investment in continuing to care for them, making this a primary concern in his life, this also requires monitoring in the minds of all adults concerned. The capacity to 'divide' equally the care of children and the small adjustments of daily life, carried out simultaneously with the process of continuing to separate from a divorced partner, often stretches parental management abilities and reserves of patience to the limit. A non-resident father may continue to behave in ways that complicate the daily smooth running of life for a child (as mother sees it) by insisting on involvement at every level of child care, such as a requirement that they be telephoned if the child has a temperature or an unexpected school outing. Such intensive preoccupation may become a habit and continue long after the child themselves experiences this as 'care'. Coresidence can lead to similar problems where either parent does not trust the other to manage the child in their absence, and continually presents themselves as outraged because some small detail of the child's life has passed unreported. The illusions created by the philosophy of 'shared care' can deny the reality that a separation has taken place, and can trap some parents and children in lives that are inappropriately tied down into detailed timetables. This can replace active thought about a child's developmental needs.

In entering these debates as professionals, we have taken the position that the conflict of interests between a parent's needs for closeness and continuity with a child, and a child's need for spontaneity cannot always be easily resolved. Much of our time has focused on helping parents to re-think some of the battles over times, spaces and activities in which they have become emotionally and psychologically entrenched. Our goal has been to open parents' minds to the effect of these battles on the children's minds and ability to think. Such battles can become centred around the essential trivia of everyday life in ways that allow us to enter and unpick the processes involved alongside their emotional meanings. An 11-year-old girl, Carlotta, for example, wanted to get some new underwear from her favourite chain store after school on Friday, and tentatively wanted to try out some bras, an activity which she preferred to do with her mother (who was working full-time and could only manage to go shopping on a Friday). However, to do this on a Friday would mean eating into her father's time with her, which technically began when school ended. Neither parent would budge or consider any lateral solutions. They had reached a position of non-negotiation over details as small as this because they each experienced the other's expression of parental involvement as intrusive and violating their own capacity to think for their child, a battle in which they each involved their new partners as 'advocates' for the rightness of their own position. In creating a neutral situation where the two of them met as Carlotta's own parents, the focus was moved to their joint mutual concern about Carlotta and her best interests as a girl of 11. This led after several meetings, alone and together, to them being able to smile a little ruefully at themselves and acknowledge that her growth towards puberty and her strengthening voice as a young adolescent needed more attention than their own self-justification.

This competitive aspect of post-divorce family management, particularly where parents interpret 'shared care' as 'exactly equal', is likely to increase as more young fathers who are separated simultaneously demonstrate a wish to continue committed fathering to their children. To avoid negative effects for children requires ongoing thought at more than one level of theorising about family life and its changes. The many ways that children's sense of security can be affected has not received wide public attention and has tended to be the preserve of researchers or journalists who may then become labelled as social alarmists. Given the number of divorces involving very young children, we hope to contribute to wider public and professional debate around the issues for children created by 'joint parenting apart'.

A child coming to terms with a newly-forming second family household, and managing the social and emotional adaptations involved, may alternatively be exposed on contact visits to a parallel experience of a 'helpless' father, who is not managing to construct a successful life either on his own or with another person. This can become a significant emotional burden. We have had to consider situations of possible harm for children (see Chapter 6) and the effects of sexual abuse for girls who had been abused either on contact visits, or while living with their father on their own. It is always important for professionals of all disciplines to note the delicate boundary that exists between a child maintaining contact that supports the relationship with a parent who may be depressed or abusing drugs or alcohol, and the risk to the child. While there is an assumption that the child will benefit from continued contact with the absent parent, this can always be changed if the child's interests indicate otherwise (Hall, 1997).

Stepsiblings and half-siblings

Many children moving into second families may also find they are taking on complex relationships with stepsiblings which change their own definition of themselves as having a 'particular place' in the family, like oldest sister or youngest brother. Newly-arriving half-siblings may compound feelings of estrangement and create complexities of family organization for particular children in which they may feel squeezed out.

Liz and Bill, Frank and Freddie, Tom and Dan, and Sheila and Roddie

When Liz and Dan separated after cohabiting for five years and having two sons, Dan took the eldest son Tom to live with him. In reflecting on this decision some two years later, Tom, then aged nine, said 'I had a hot line to his heart and he to mine'. The younger son, Bill, went to live with his mother and her new partner, Frank, whom she subsequently married. In Frank's family, a son with serious learning disabilities took up a large part of the family concern's about time and management. Bill and Tom both took warmly to their new step-brother and joined in the rotas of care involved when he was at home. Initially, Bill as well as Tom felt secure in the knowledge that he had his own father's love. He visited Dan and Tom regularly every other weekend. Difficulties arose, however, when a new baby, Roddy, was born in father's household. Dan and his partner Sheila, Roddy's mother, began to argue every time Bill visited as she said that he took up too much space which was now needed for the new baby. Bill was very distressed by these arguments and felt very responsible for causing so many rows. The situation was 'resolved' by Bill sharing a room with Roddy, who woke him up as babies do at all hours of the night. This affected his ability in the school athletic programme at which he had been excelling. The fact that the baby 's needs came before his own in Sheila and Dan's home became accentuated when one-half of the room in which he and Roddy slept was painted up for the baby, and his half was left unpainted on the basis that as a teenager he would prefer to decorate it himself with posters and other wall coverings. Bill described this as quite a rejection but was keen not to make a fuss about it as it had reduced the quarreling between his dad and Roddy's mum about his visits. However, the subtle disqualification of himself as a significant person to his father began to show in other ways, so that he allowed himself to be bullied in situations where he had previously felt in charge. His older brother, who was increasingly fed up with the amount of attention now being lavished on baby Roddy also began to bully him when he visited, complaining that he was always hanging around and being a nuisance when Tom just wanted to be off with his teenage friends. Liz saw the brother's relationship as key to Bill's self-esteem, 'We need to build up Bill's confidence, to make him feel strong about himself and that's difficult when the person he is closest to doesn't really help him'. Conversation with all the adults in the original family, with Frank as well as with the two brothers, led to some recognition of the ways each brother felt displaced by the needs of younger and more-dependent children in both households, and to some parental adaptations.

Do new relationships break up?

We know from statistics that of those who divorce over 60 per cent remarry, and a higher percentage of remarriages break down. What remains undocumented is how many cohabitations, partnerships or 'friendship' relationships in which children begin to form close relationships with the new adult partner of their parent, also form a part of children's lives. In our experience the majority of men and women took partners in ways that involved their 'friends' or more openly declared lovers in the lives of their children. Many of these relationships ended or broke up with bitterness in the course of the years we knew them. Several mothers and fathers had relationships with new partners which ended while they were still coming to see us with their children. Of the fathers' relationships, all except one were initially hidden from the children, whereas in all cases but one the mother's relationships were known to the children. It is clearly more difficult for a woman whose children live with her to have a relationship which is concealed. In two households where there had been violence in the first marriage, the children actively contributed to mother's decision not to continue a new relationship which the children saw as a threat to their newly-secure family life at home.

However, differences among children complicated decisions further, since in one family a son wanted his mother to continue the relationship, and a daughter did not. It was clear that children carried a lot of power in relation to their mothers' decisions about whether to continue with a new lover. Where a mother had formed a relationship with another woman which subsequently broke up, the children were not always told about the sexual nature of the friendship. This was not always in their mother's best interests, as a father might hold the information as a secret bargaining tactic, to be used in one family against their mother when the children were older. In a second lesbian relationship a mother, Claire, and her partner handled a number of highly complex issues, like the death of gay menfriends who had Aids, and the children were part of this milieu early in their lives. Their father's hostile attitude to his ex-wife's lifestyle maintained our involvement with the family over a number of years. During these years Claire had number of relationships with women which were more concealed from the children. Out of all second relationship break-ups only one boy expressed sorrow that a mother had let her partner go. Having lost his own father completely at the age of three, following a violent separation, he had enjoyed the male companionship offered by his mother's boyfriend who took him swimming and played football with him. Another boy who was clearly upset by the effect on his mother of her relationship break-up responded by spending much more time with his own father and his new wife, which supported him in sustaining his mother's grief and anger. Nonetheless, this took its toll on his own functioning at school, and his sense of insecurity in his mother's household.

In detailing the variety of children's experiences hidden under the heading of 'reordering', we have included the numbers within our own group of families. Five of the fathers had girlfriends with whom they subsequently broke up, whereas a further six went on to form second families with new babies. In only one case had the child become attached to the new girlfriend, and expressed sorrow in terms of her own personal loss. Although girls expressed jealousy of father's girlfriends, where a woman made it clear to the daughter that she was not trying to threaten the daughter's relationship with her father, a child was then less likely to feel her personal position was threatened and could even enjoy the new relationship in her own right. However, there were many variations among children's expressed views. One brother and sister despised their father for having had affairs but had to come to terms with father's girlfriends working alongside him in the shop; one daughter who was distressed when her father lost his friend, became outraged when her mother told her it had been a sexual relationship. This information was given by mother to balance up father's attack on mother for taking a lover some two years after the separation. In one family, father's break-up with his girlfriend ended in the way many children long for because he returned to their mother with whom he still seemed to be very much in love.

In two families one child had gone with mother when she left the marital home, and one child had stayed with father. In each case the child who stayed with father became extremely close and protective of this mutually-caregiving experience. Each child was seen by others as behaving more like a partner than a child. Where the girl was living with her father, she subsequently became neglected when her father became involved with another woman in a drug-taking milieu. At this point her mother removed her. The son who 'looked after' his father became equally antagonistic to the idea of him marrying and was referred for physically attacking his father's new partner. He said of his father 'he should have told me and not done it behind my back'.

A positive attitude towards children was regarded as a highly important factor in all mothers' decisions to live with a new partner, but it was usually a secondary issue for the men who had left home for another woman. A number of mothers who had been 'left' continued to behave as though father's new partner was of little relevance to the children, which made it more difficult for the children to relate to the new woman in their lives in realistic ways. They continued to be organised by a sense of loyalty to their mothers in recognition of her sadness. While the majority of incoming adults were seen by the child's parents as 'doing their best for them', some, confronted with the reality of the children's ambivalent or anxious attitudes towards them, behaved in ways that became persistently critical or hostile. This vulnerable period in reordered family formation can often be a time when all the resentments about the divorce having occurred were acted out by the children, and, in a small number of the families we saw, these resentments between children and their stepparent lasted for many years. However, when a stepparent took a strong positive line towards a child, they had a powerful effect in improving the child's sense of self-esteem and in enabling them to manage other difficult aspects of the post-divorce situation.

Gerald, whose own father maintained a constant vigilant and jealous eye on mother's new relationship, found that his mother's new partner Liam offered a warm and calm alternative to his volatile parents and their ongoing dramatic post-divorce relationship. He spent time playing ball games with Gerald, doing homework in a quiet situation, and took him on outings to visit his large and welcoming family. He also taught Gerald ways of handling his own angry feelings by discouraging him from swearing and being abusive to others, a form of behaviour which had led him into further trouble at school. Over two years, Gerald's improved behaviour and school performance, as well as increased football skills, brought their own rewards and, interacting with his sense of a welcoming male presence in the home, led to an improvement in his own self-esteem.

An important stress factor for children was the ongoing experience of a highly critical parent or stepparent. Six of the mothers in our study maintained a persistently critical commentary on their children. In two of those families the stepfathers also took a critical position, and a further three fathers often ran their children down or criticised them inappropriately in front of them. Just as it is difficult to disentangle the effects of divorce from the effects of quarreling and violence, or persistent family discord, it is also difficult to assess the relative harm done by a particular life event like parental break-up in distinction from the ongoing damage done to the self-image of the child by a parent or stepparent who persistently runs the child down. Where a parent has a tendency to be critical towards a child, and is themself struggling to manage a family under difficult circumstances, criticism is likely to be increased. A good relationship with a stepparent appeared to act as a moderating factor in terms of positive development: this could be seen happening in three families. Conversely, a bad relationship could amplify already existing vulnerabilities, increase low self-esteem, and lead to reactive rather than thought-out behaviour on the young person's part. This was clearly happening in two families where the stepfathers were maintaining a critical stance towards the children which amplified a critical position taken by the mother.

An earlier study (Gorell Barnes et al., 1998) has shown that a stepparent who moderates unhappiness or discord in the home into which they enter, can, through the quality of the relationship with their partner, set up small changes for the better which amplify over time. This former study gave some vivid examples of how small and regular commitments to aspects of the children's lives can also make a difference. Such changes occurred both between stepparent and child, and in the relationship between the children in the household. In the long term this may then result in young people leaving home in less dramatic and reactive ways, an aspect of leaving home which has been shown to distinguish stepfamilies from intact biological families or lone-parent families. Cutting off connections is likely to be more hazardous for young people who have already had a connection with a parent disrupted or severed following divorce. A stepparent who aggravates already-existing discordant or unhappy relationships within a post-divorce family can therefore amplify risks for the children, and precipitate them into premature independence which carries its own dangers (Kiernan, 1992; Jones, 1995).

However, in this current study we knew the children's second families at a time where bonds were only tenuously being formed, often in the face of opposition (open and hidden) from the children's other parent. Many of the difficulties and problems reported as arising in stepfamilies arise from the complexities of relationship transitions we have briefly described, and in particular from the demands of moving from one set of family loyalties to beginning new attachments. Such transitions contain losses, and where these losses go unacknowledged and undiscussed between parents and children they can create cumulative stress. Whatever the gains to come, the breaking up of marriage disrupts former intimate relationships and patterns of stability and attachment for children. For children who go through more than one parental or stepparental break-up, the cumulative losses may become harder to sustain without impaired health or impaired social or emotional development. We know that at least one-sixth of parents who divorce, divorce a second time. For some children, therefore, the process of transition will be an ongoing part of their lives. Whether or not this makes it easier to accommodate to further change, and whether change itself becomes a factor for accumulated stress leading to disturbance, is not yet sufficiently described and discussed. Dunn *et al.* (1999) have mounted a large-scale study of changing relationships in family life from which some further answers to questions of cumulative transition and what creates the conditions for successful adaptation may emerge.

Summary

Second families and childrens' resilience

The following are some of the factors we think it important for parents and professionals to look out for on behalf of children in reordered families:

- At a time of parental repartnering, feelings of disloyalty to the divorced 'other parent' may be rearoused in the children. The nature of ongoing ties and what happens to adult love and commitment may come up for discussion.
- Children need time to process the fact that their parent is taking a new partner, and to think about some of the possible effects on their own lives. Children who have lived alone with a parent for some time may in addition feel they are being displaced by an incoming adult. It is better to give time and discussion for such feelings than dismissing them as foolish.
- A child may need help in thinking how he can stay connected to his own father or mother and still have affection for an adult who acts as a partner to his mum or dad.
- Stepfamilies need time to establish themselves and their new patterns of living together.
- Emotional experience in stepfamilies, and particularly children's experiences, need to be understood in contexts other than the immediate family. These include all the previous transitions, including the effects of the break-up of the first marriage. Research has shown how such effects continue into life in reordered families, and suggests that more time Should be given to thinking about the impact of earlier relationships on what may be going on in the life of the second marriage and family.
- Earlier relationships and their negative effects may continue to be present in reordered families where children have regular contact with a parent who remains in conflict with their residential parent. Time and thought need to be given to how the boundary between families is best maintained on behalf of the child.

- As children will have to learn to manage a number of very different parental expectations, they will need time and patience in talking through the ways these may affect them.
- Persistent unresolved quarreling, violence or abuse carry powerful legacies for children. Children may need help to prevent their own self-esteem being undermined.

8

THE SCHOOL: A SECURE BASE?

Teachers in loco parentis

The relationship between families and schools spans a considerable period of the family life-cycle (Dowling and Osborne,1994).
During this period the teachers are entrusted with responsibility
for the children, but will have varying degrees of knowledge
about events at home which are affecting the children's development and state of mind. Considerable responsibility can be placed
on teachers when the family is in crisis, although they are often
not prepared for it. In the face of the increasing demise of local
services, parents tend to use the school as the first port of call to
share family crises and sometimes the expectations placed on
teachers far exceed their ability to respond to parents in distress.
(Personal communication from a primary headteacher.)

Family transitions are for the most part known to the school via
the children. Exciting news such as moving house, the arrival of a
new baby in the family, extended-family visitors and so on, are
brought to the teachers' attention by the children and have a connotation of pride and happiness. However, in the minds of the
children, certain family events are best kept secret as they are
associated with unhappiness, conflict and, implicitly, shame as
children see themselves as part of it. Divorce as a family transition
is one such event and carries with it a complex web of emotions
which makes it difficult to communicate and share in the way
that a 'happy event' might be shared. Children may experience a
mixture of relief – if divorce represents the end of a violent or
abusive relationship – and a sense of loss for what cannot be any
longer. The loss of the intact family as an ideal, however unsatis-
factory as a reality, is a powerful experience for children of all
ages. For some families, separation and divorce may be the end of

a long road of unhappiness, prolonged conflict and arguments and a climate of tension at home. In parallel, the life children have at school carries its own pleasures and demands, and implies an expectation that structures at home are in place to support the child's work at school.

The pre-school years

The relationship between parents and teachers also has a life-cycle of its own. At the pre-school stage it is expected – and understood – that parents will be involved with the children in the nursery. The boundaries between home and school are much more permeable and parents float in and out of the classroom helping their children to 'settle in', or helping in a more general way with the activities. The nursery teacher is often seen by the parents as mainly a nurture figure, a substitute mother who will help the child socialise, get used to other children and develop certain skills in preparation for 'big school'.

Expectations about the role of the nursery school teacher will vary according to the parents' views and beliefs about the purpose of nursery education. For some it will perhaps be a chance for the parent to have a break, or to attend to a younger sibling. The expectations will centre around the opportunity for the child to learn to cope with separation from mother for a few hours, 'getting used' to other children and learning some useful skills. Parents will have a range of expectations regarding the teaching/learning aspect of the nursery, and some would regard the playing and socialising as insufficient in terms of what they would see as the task of a nursery school teacher.

Some parents, particularly if they come from different cultures and ethnic groups, may regard the nursery as a place of acculturation for their child, where they will learn the language and develop new skills. Some of these families may depend on the school to provide their children with the skills to manage the new culture, and as the children become more competent in the language some parents rely on them to communicate with the school on their behalf. In some cases the children have to cope with a conflict of roles within the family structure which may be difficult to manage. On the one hand they will be expected to depend on the parents and to comply with rules and discipline. On the other hand they will be given the authority to communicate with the school on the parents' behalf, thus experiencing the parents' dependency on their competence to relate to the outside world.

From the children's perspective, the nursery school will provide a world of discovery and excitement which will be approached with a mixture of interest and apprehension, and to which the child will adapt more or less well according to their previous experiences of secure or anxious attachment (see Chapter 2).

Pre-school and parental break-up

Billy used to arrive with his father every morning to the nursery. He would come in confidently and grab the grey donkey, a familiar object which he had taken a liking to since his first day. Then, he would glance back at his father and, either run back for a quick hug, or just wave with the kind of confidence indicating that he had arrived in familiar territory and he would be all right. His father would wait just long enough to ensure that this was so, glancing a bit nervously at the other children and the teacher and helper, as if to reassure himself that they would all know what to do if Billy suddenly became distressed. Occasionally the teacher would glance back at him and indicate that all would be well. But even if she didn't, Billy's father did know when it was safe for him to leave. This complex web of verbal and non-verbal signals, exchanged almost imperceptibly and with not much thinking in between, had evolved since the beginning of term and the predictability of the signs has reassured everyone involved that if they are read correctly all will be well; that is, Billy will be fine until lunch time when his mother will collect him. Billy himself seemed very comfortable with that routine and gradually branched out to experiment with different toys and play with different children.

The first day after half term Billy didn't come to the nursery. On the Tuesday he arrived with his mother. It wasn't the usual confident Billy going straight to the grey donkey. He was hiding behind his mother and sucking a bit of cloth he had brought with him. His mother skirted around the nursery, dragging Billy behind her, hoping to catch the teacher's eye. She looked drained and tired. The teacher was busy comforting Lucy who had hurt herself on the slide. However, she soon noticed the unfamiliar sight of sad looking Billy and his mother. A conversation ensued, a brief explanation was given, it was difficult to talk in front of Billy; Father had left, it had all been very difficult. The teacher tried to help Billy engage with the toys and move him on to take part in the ongoing activities which after a while he was able to do. He joined the story corner. By then, his mother felt she had said enough, and feeling rather embarrassed she left quickly without waiting for the teacher to return ...

This, and similar scenarios, will be familiar to most teachers. What was said, what was not said, Billy's behaviour, will all have to be put together by the teacher in order to make sense of what is going on for Billy.

Different teachers will have different reactions to the situation described above. However, most of them will feel the need to develop strategies to cope with the changes in behaviour of children like Billy, with the parents who may or may not approach them directly, and with the rest of the children in the class. At a pre-school level the relationship between parents and teachers is quite close and it should be possible for the teacher to offer support to both parent and child. However, how realistic is it, both in terms of time and skill required, for the nursery teacher to respond in a way that is appropriate, without becoming a counsellor or a social worker and without feeling left with a range of powerful feelings and not quite knowing what to do next?

Ideally there should be systems in place in schools for teachers to have an opportunity to discuss children who are worrying them. Educational psychologists provide a valuable resource but their time is limited and much of it is taken up with the assessment of special educational needs. Mental health professionals who provide consultation to schools, as in the example below, are also a valuable resource. However, for the most part, teachers encounter situations such as Billy's as part of their daily work and have to draw on their own resources to manage such situations. The nursery teacher can be of considerable help to the child *in the context of the classroom* by:

- Keeping communication open. It is important for nursery teachers to make sure that parents inform them of any changes in children's routines. Likewise it is useful for parents to know of any changes in the child's behaviour in the nursery.
- Acknowledging changes in circumstances for the child and normalising them. It will be an enormous relief for children like Billy and his parents if the teacher acknowledges that

from now on it will be Billy's mother who brings him to school but on certain days his father will collect him.

- Making sure *both parents* are informed of any school events.
- If necessary, teachers should not hesitate to ask the parents to come in, either together or separately, to discuss their child.
- Reporting any concerns to the head teacher in order for appropriate action to be taken.
- Recognising their own anxieties and making sure there is an opportunity to discuss them and share them in order to get appropriate support.
- Being very clear of the boundaries between what they *can and cannot do* in their role as teachers.

The primary school years

'I forgot my PE kit because I was at my dad's last night' is a straightforward enough excuse. However, for the child it carries the connotation of responsibility for keeping together the two worlds created by their parents' decision to separate. There is no preparation or training for such a massive change in family life. As the expectation for most children is that the conflict, however serious, will eventually be resolved and the parents will remain together, family breakdown happens rather suddenly from their point of view.

As explained in Chapter 2, the two worlds of home and school are held together in the child's mind and what happens in one context is constantly having an impact on the other. The structure of a primary school in the UK fosters the relationship with an 'attachment figure' in the school context. There is one class teacher for each year, and children spend the majority of their learning time with him or her. Helpers who provide additional input in the classroom are all secondary to the main relationship with the class teacher. In the infant school the boundaries between home and school are quite permeable. Parents come into the classroom and some provide help with reading and other activities. Therefore, it ought to be possible, at least in theory, for teachers to be aware of the changing circumstances in family life which may be affecting the child's daily behaviour at school.

Current political pressures on teachers – league tables, standard-ised tests, 'attainment targets' – persistently ignore the constant interaction of family and school contexts and their effect on children's performance. A commonly held assumption is that if only teachers tried harder or used the 'right' methods, the children would perform better. This oversimplification represents an attempt on the part of society to charge the teachers with the responsibility for improving single-handedly what is often a result of complex influences on a child's development. There is a persistent attempt to stress the need for academic performance and cognitive devel-opment whilst neglecting the emotional factors which affect children's capacity for learning.

A primary school teacher, Miss S, consulted me over the difficulty a seven-year-old boy was having with reading. Despite the teacher's spe-cial efforts and the fact that Joe was having additional input twice a week in a small group, he was not making any progress; in fact Miss S thought he was going backwards. She seemed mystified by this as she considered Joe an intelligent boy who liked school and was keen to learn. During the consultation I tried to explore in some detail what exactly was the diffi-culty with reading. The teacher explained that Joe found it difficult to 'anticipate what was coming' in the text and had difficulty with 'sequencing'. I became curious about what was going on in Joe's life and the teacher found it freeing to talk about Joe and his family as she had tried everything 'educational' already. In fact she was very knowledge-able about current reading theories but had not had the opportunity to explore connections between Joe's family and emotional context, and his learning at school.

She told me that Joe's mum and dad had separated nine months ago. Since then mum had entered higher education. Doing a degree plus run-ning a home single-handed had put considerable pressures on her. Although the separation had been acrimonious, the parents had reached a stage in their relationship where they were able to cooperate and help one another in the sharing of Joe's care. However, due to the nature of Joe's father's work, arrangements were erratic, often made at the last min-ute and, in the teacher's words, Joe would often not know who would pick him up from school or whose house he was going to at the end of the day. 'He can't anticipate what is going to happen to him', were the teacher's words. I made the connection between the difficulty in anticip-ating what was coming each day, and what was coming next in the text when reading. We thought together about how difficult it was for Joe to think about 'what was coming next' when life was so unpredictable. The teacher found this connection helpful and we thought together of ways in which life could become a little more predictable for Joe. I suggested a meeting with the parents, but Miss S volunteered that this had proved quite difficult before. Mother tended to pop in at the beginning of the school day when she dropped Joe off, and at that time it was difficult for the teacher to enter into a detailed discussion. Father had never made it to parents' evenings, so the teacher had tried once or twice to send a note with Joe asking him to come in the next day but had had no response.

We decided that perhaps helping the parents to plan in advance for the meeting might make it easier to attend. The teacher had not thought of seeing them together but was willing to try. We agreed to write a letter to both of them inviting them to meet with me and the teacher to think about Joe's reading. However, we soon discovered the school did not have father's address. Maybe he never knew about parents' evenings! After some efforts on the part of the teacher, we were able to write to both parents. They both came. Father was delighted to come in. He had assumed that the school always communicated with mother, and the notes asking him to come in the next day had felt like a 'telling off', so he had ignored them, just as he used to when he was told off at school.

The meeting made him feel that both parents were valued at school, and the fact that he had been given enough notice allowed him to plan to attend. Both parents understood how difficult it was for Joe, and for the school, not to know what was happening at the end of the day, but conveyed to us their difficulties in planning in advance in the context of their busy lives.

We agreed that it would at least be possible to plan for the week ahead. The parents agreed to talk on Sunday evening and decide who was doing what from Monday to Friday. The parent who had Joe that Sunday would write it down and show it to Joe. Each parent agreed to do 10 minutes reading with Joe at a set time once a week. The teacher and the parents agreed to meet again a month later to review progress. A follow up consultation revealed that Joe's reading was improving and he was particularly enjoying reading with his father on Wednesdays after swimming.

The teacher as a secure base

School can be the one place which offers stability and predictability at a time of family transition and turmoil. However, children often find it difficult to share family circumstances particularly if this is going to make them feel different from their peers. Mitchell (1985) holds the view that it is easier for children if teachers sensitively approach them when they suspect family problems: in her study she found that children who appeared to feel isolated and bewildered at school would have liked the teacher to approach them. Frieman (1993) stresses that a valuable tool for teachers is to let the child know discreetly they are willing to listen. However, teachers may feel reluctant to get involved in these issues or do not feel equipped to deal with the emotional intensity that may be generated. Others do not see it as their job (Cox and Desforges, 1987).

Despite the recognition in the literature that divorce and separation can have an effect on children's learning and adjustment to school, there has been no research seeking the views of teachers and others involved in the educational process. Two small studies carried out by our postgraduate students have sought to explore teachers' and educational psychologists' views regarding the role of the school in relation to children of divorced parents (McNab, 1993; Blacher, 1997). Both studies found that there were no consistent school policies in relation to separated parents, and different schools managed it in different ways, often relying on individual teacher's interest and initiatives. Teachers varied in their view of their role and what they could do to help the children. Broadly speaking there were those who believed that they could and should play a role, both in supporting the child and actively seeking to communicate with parents, particularly the non-resident parent, in order to ensure that they were kept informed of their children's progress. Others preferred to wait and be approached by the parent.

Growing up – transition to secondary school

This important transition for children has long been recognised in the education literature (J. Dowling, 1980, 1986; Youngman, 1986). For the children it constitutes a change which will in most cases be regarded with a mixture of apprehension and excitement. Their views and beliefs about the school they are going to will be influenced by what they know about it, whether other friends are going, whether there has been a choice and they felt part of it, whether they have siblings already attending, and many other features of the school such as distance, size, whether coeducational or single sex, and so on.

For the parents, many of those variables will play a part in their choice of school for their child. In our experience the overriding consideration from the parents' point of view is whether a particular school feels right for *their* child. This judgement will be based on any one or many of the above features. For some parents the primary concern will be the academic standards, for others it will be emphasis on discipline, location, quality of teaching or a combination of many factors usually referred to as the schools 'reputation' or 'ethos'.

Amongst the many changes affecting children when they transfer to secondary school will be the experience of having to relate to many more adults in the course of the school day. The relationship with the class teacher as 'attachment figure' which existed in the primary school will be replaced by relationships with a number of teachers in different roles. Schools with sound pastoral care systems will ensure that there is a key figure who will provide continuity for the child, usually the form tutor and/ or head of year, who in some schools continue with that particular group of children up to year 11. Nevertheless, the features of a large secondary school can be overwhelming. Carrying your books from one room to the next, managing to remember the timetable and who to speak to about different things, relating to new peers as well as adults, and coping with the pressures of lessons in different subjects as well as the expectations of different teachers regarding homework and standards of behaviour, is a tall order for a 12-year-old.

Despite all these demands, we know that most children adapt and are able to learn and develop not only academically but socially and emotionally during the secondary school years. However, we also know that a significant proportion of children experience emotional and behavioural difficulties and many fail to achieve their potential despite the school's efforts. Some truant persistently, and an increasing number are getting excluded from school. Again, the oversimplified solutions often put forward by politicians suggest that if teachers only taught better all would be well. Workers in the mental health, education, social services and primary care fields know from experience how often complex factors contribute to children failing to achieve at school.

Divorce and the secondary school

Between the ages of 11 and 16, children are developing significant relationships with their peers and struggling with forming a sense of identity separate from their family of origin, although they retain strong emotional links with their parents (Hill, 1989). When a major transition such as the divorce of the parents occurs, it represents a significant disruption in the young person's life which makes it very difficult to concentrate on school work and may have repercussions on the way they see themselves in their social context. Children may act-out to seek attention, or try to identify very strongly with the peer culture in order to distance themselves from the parental conflict. Conversely they may become very preoccupied with parenting the parents, at the expense of their own emotional and social development.

Anna was a cheerful, enthusiastic year-10 pupil. She attended a girl's school where the emphasis was not only on academic achievement but the school was committed to the social and emotional development of the girls. There was a strong pastoral care system, teachers spent time thinking about the pupils, and the school had effective channels of communication if things went wrong.

Anna was on course to get good grades at GCSE. English was one of her strongest subjects and she enjoyed creative writing and having a go at poetry. Anna also had a very good relationship with her English teacher, in whom she had confided once or twice. The teacher, a gifted and sensitive individual, struggled at times with the boundary between being a 'confidante' for the girls and being able to assert her authority when she needed to make demands in terms of homework, punctuality and the standard of work. It came as a shock to her to read one of Anna's essays just before the Easter holidays. It was a very depressing story which depicted the main character, a girl of Anna's age as wanting to kill herself, feeling unloved and hating her stepfather. The teacher became quite anxious and her dilemma was: if she were to take this story as autobiographical, and therefore a cry for help from Anna, she should take action, talk to the parents, talk to the Head, 'do something'. On the other hand, she *was only an English teacher*, what right had she to infer anything from the girl's essay. The teacher discussed this dilemma with one of us and we came to the conclusion that it was possible to raise her concern with the parents *in the context of discussing the content of Anna's English work*. Her attempts to engage in discussion with either parent resulted in a rather fraught dialogue where she experienced a lot of pressure to reassure the parents that Anna would get an A in her GCSE. The teacher was left feeling dejected and impotent, wondering if anyone other than her was worried about Anna's distress.

She brought up her concern in the context of a group consultation offered by one of us on a regular basis to the school. The group offered ideas and support, and a number of possible strategies were explored. The teacher felt empowered to tackle the parents but the group agreed that the deputy Head, with responsibility for pastoral care, should join her. During the course of the group's work, the boundaries between what teachers can and cannot do became clearer. For example, when discussing issues about eating disorders, they evolved a policy of requiring medical certificates prior to school journeys for those girls whose health caused concern. They also became more confident about asking parents to take responsibility for their children when they were unwell.

What schools can do

The development of a school policy

A clear policy regarding seeking information from parents in relation to major family transitions would result in useful information being available to teachers: for example both the addresses at which the child now lives, as well as days when children go to each parent.

When parents have separate addresses, a policy of contacting *both* parents for *all* events, from parents' evenings to social events, sports days, jumble sales and so on would convey to the parents an active wish on the part of the school to remain in communication with both of them. At a time when parents' self-esteem may be low and they are having doubts about the right thing to do in relation to the children, active communication from the school would reflect the belief that *both parents* are important regardless of their changing family circumstances. This active effort on the part of the school is more likely to enable parents to feel secure enough to come forward with information about their changing circumstances, and would then result in parents and teachers working cooperatively for the benefit of the children rather than children having to act as 'go-betweens', feeling responsible for passing information from one to the other.

It must be remembered that at the time of divorce parents may be feeling vulnerable and anxious, but also that the relationship between them will be difficult and often the level of conflict will be considerable. Therefore, the knowledge that the school has systems in place to deal with *all* separated parents, not just them, will be a great relief and will hopefully help them in their relationship with the school to the benefit of the children.

Parents' evenings

This is the opportunity for parents to hear about their children's progress and schools must ensure that both parents, whatever their circumstances, feel able to attend and contribute. On the whole, parents manage to come together for such events particularly when the child has ongoing contact with both parents. However, there may be situations where the level of conflict is so high that the parents don't want to be in the same place at the same time. It ought to be possible for schools to have some flexibility which would allow parents to see teachers separately. This is of course placing even more demands on extremely busy teachers, but such gestures of goodwill could be enormously beneficial in terms of allowing that parent to remain connected to their child's school and to believe that they continue to be important in their child's life.

In a secondary school, where it would prove impractical to organise yet another meeting with all the teachers, the opportunity to meet with the form tutor or year head who would convey the views of the subject teachers to the parent could be an indication that it really mattered to the school to remain in contact with both parents.

Training for teachers

The experience of separation and divorce brings about a range of intense feelings of sadness, anger, loss, guilt and regret as well as hopes and expectations for the future. This increasingly common life transition may have touched the teachers' experience either in their current families or in their families of origin. Their own experiences will colour and inform their views and beliefs about divorce and its effects on children. Teachers need opportunities to examine their own beliefs and ideas about these effects, and to learn about current findings on the subject. In-service training opportunities should be made available on this and other family transitions.

What teachers can do

Curriculum

Teachers have always been able to incorporate relevant issues into the curriculum through making relevant connections for the children. Current policies such as the National Curriculum should, in principle, make it possible for teachers to include the different family forms by using examples of family life to reflect the current variations in society. This will help the children not to feel alienated by not having the ideal nuclear family (Gorrell Barnes, 1998). Other authors support this view: according to Ayalon and Flasher (1993), the family is often portrayed in the curriculum only in the traditional pattern of father, mother and biological children, which deprives children of examining issues of different family relationships in the context of the peer group. Pecherek (1996) suggests schools can support pupils by ensuring that teaching materials reflect different family forms which the children can relate to their own situation, rather than emphasising the normality of the 'nuclear' family. Cockett and Tripp (1994) consider this would allow children to feel better about themselves and improve their self image, which would in turn contribute to breaking the cycle of underachievement that affects some of these children.

The pastoral care system should make it possible for children to share family transitions with a designated member of staff they can trust and who is known to the children as someone who can be available to them should they need to talk. Teachers can play a very supportive role by sensitively letting the child know that they are willing to listen (Frieman, 1993). However, not all children will be comfortable talking about what they feel is a private issue (McNab, 1993). Many have mixed feelings about their family circumstances becoming common knowledge, and most children have a strong wish not to be seen as different from their peers (Mitchell, 1985).

The Personal and Social Education lessons in secondary schools provide an ideal opportunity to promote group discussion on issues related to life transitions in general, and separation and divorce in particular. To bring these issues into the classroom domain will give a strong message to the children that it is acceptable and worthwhile talking about such life events and their impact on young people. Teachers responsible for home and school liaison, year heads, special needs coordinators, support teachers, and others with pastoral responsibility, by virtue of their special role may be particularly aware of changes in family circumstances. They are in a good position to ensure the school responds sensitively to these changes.

When to seek outside help

The ways in which the school can attend and be sensitive to issues of divorce and separation affecting the children have been outlined above. However, there will always be situations which teachers will consider inappropriate to deal with themselves, preferring to call on outside professionals to help.

Teachers are often at the receiving end of manifestations of disturbance in children which have been triggered off by a family transition. Children suddenly becoming aggressive, withdrawn, losing interest in work and erratic in attendance are but some of the signs which can become apparent when there is turmoil at home. Other more persistent and perhaps longer-term difficulties such as eating disorders can also become exacerbated by family crises. There are situations where teachers feel they have done all they can for the child they are concerned about and it may be appropriate to refer to a specialist service. Referrals can be made to the school psychological service, child and family consultation services, or social services as appropriate. The roles of different professionals in relation to children of divorcing families will be more fully examined in Chapter 10.

Family–school consultation

In those situations where there are issues for the school in terms of the child's attainment or behaviour, it is useful to offer family–school consultation at the school. Such intervention facilitates communication between parents and teachers who together can explore new ways of handling the child's difficulties. The following are two examples:

Mark's primary school was having difficulty coping with him and had threatened to exclude him if his behaviour did not improve. At the age of nine Mark had already changed schools five times and, given the turmoil he had been through in his family life during his parents' long and acrimonious separation period, it seemed important to preserve continuity in the school context for him.

A meeting was set up at the school with the head teacher, Mark's class teacher, the educational psychologist for the school who had assessed Mark, Mark's mother and one of us. The meeting started with a catalogue of complaints about Mark's behaviour in the classroom and at play time: he was aggressive towards other children, disruptive and constantly seeking attention from the teacher. This behaviour had set in motion a circular pattern whereby the more attention Mark sought, the more exasperated the teacher became as she had 30 children to attend to. Mark then resorted to disruptive behaviour which at least got him negative attention. However, he felt very miserable as he was constantly rejected and ostracised by his classmates. During the meeting it was very painful for Mark's mother to listen to all the complaints. She knew what it was like to cope with Mark's aggression, she had been at the receiving end of it. Nevertheless, it felt excruciating to hear yet again that the school would not tolerate him any longer. The teachers for their part had tried everything they could, and particularly the class teacher felt at the end of her tether. We established that the most difficult part of the day was lunch time play, when Mark's aggressive behaviour became unmanageable for the dinner ladies.

The suggestion that maybe the school needed a break, and Mark should go home for lunch was welcomed by the teachers but not by mother who was working part of the week. We were able to find a compromise and agreed that Mark would be taken home for lunch three days a week. This partial solution enabled the teachers to feel that they were sharing the responsibility with Mark's mother. She, in turn, felt supported by the school who were prepared to continue having Mark for the rest of the academic year. Mark felt relieved as he got very anxious when the long break at lunch time approached. He knew no one would play with him and therefore resorted to aggressive behaviour and name-calling which in turn provoked further rejection by his peers.

We also agreed that the educational psychologist would meet with the class teacher on a regular basis and develop strategies for managing Mark in the classroom.

In the following example, a secondary school consultation provided a setting where divorced parents could focus together on their daughter's education:

Francesca was due to transfer to secondary school in the autumn term. Although her parents had separated several years ago, they still disagreed about most things to do with the upbringing of Francesca, and she was constantly keeping the peace between them, often by sacrificing her own views and wishes. Decisions about secondary transfer had brought conflict to the fore yet again. The teachers in Francesca's primary school were concerned about her attainment, and in the past she had been described as 'dyslexic'.

A meeting was convened at the school to review Francesca's emotional and academic needs and to discuss options for secondary transfer. As we had been involved in work with the family, one of us was invited to attend and was impressed by the care and concern expressed by the staff in relation to Francesca. The class teacher had prepared a careful report of Francesca's achievements in class during the last term. The special-needs coordinator, although still concerned about her maths and spelling, reported an improvement in Francesca's reading which left only a few months discrepancy between reading age and chronological age.

Francesca's main problem, from the teacher's point of view, was her low self-esteem and her difficulty in believing in herself and her abilities. Parents and teachers agreed that there had been sufficient improvement for Francesca not to be labelled 'dyslexic'. [No one seemed to know where the label had come from.] We all agreed it was important to ensure Francesca got feedback about her improvements and focus on her strengths. She should be encouraged not to think of herself as a dyslexic pupil. Teachers and parents also commented on the strategies Francesca was developing to improve her spelling.

During the discussion it was remarkable to see how both parents were cooperating with one another in the context of thinking what was best for their daughter. In this climate of cooperation it was possible to move on to discuss transfer to secondary school and keep the focus on *where Francesca's needs would be best met.* With the help of the teachers and their knowledge of what different schools would offer, it was possible to explore options and for the parents to abandon their very entrenched beliefs about which was the 'best school'. At follow-up a year later, the parents reported Francesca was doing well and enjoying her secondary school. She was receiving no special help. The parents were more able to talk to each other without arguing, and there was no conflict regarding contact arrangements.

As the examples above illustrate, it is important for teachers to be clear about the boundaries around what they can and cannot do in school. It can be useful to have a neutral outsider to facilitate discussions with parents in those instances where situations have become so polarised and positions are so entrenched that it is quite difficult to explore different options.

Another option for teachers is to have opportunities to discuss children who are worrying them by meeting as a group with a facilitator who might be an educational psychologist or a professional from a child and family mental health agency.

Summary

Key points for teachers

- Keep communication with parents open.
- Make sure both parents are informed of school events.
- If necessary, ask parents to come in together or separately to discuss their child.
- Report any concerns to the head teacher.
- Recognise own anxieties and ensure there is opportunity to discuss them.
- Be clear about the boundaries between what a teacher can and cannot do.

Schools need to

- Develop appropriate school policies regarding family transitions.

- As far as possible, ensure that both parents have access to parents' evenings and information about children's progress.
- Develop ways of widening the curriculum to address a variety of family structures.
- Develop a pastoral care system which enables children to develop a relationship of trust with a designated member of staff.
- Put in place support systems for the staff to share their anxieties and concerns about pupils.
- Develop relationships with specialist services in order to be able to refer pupils and to request support for the staff as appropriate.

9

DIVORCE AND PRIMARY HEALTH CARE

The primary care context

General practitioners are at the front-line of the primary care service. Their relationship with patients and their families may span across the family life-cycle, and in the more stable communities there probably will be an intergenerational relationship. They are therefore more likely than any other professional to hear about – and intervene – when a family transition occurs. The distress, upheaval and often conflict-laden situation surrounding the process of separation or divorce may not be, in the eyes of the parents, 'serious' enough to warrant a referral to what in the NHS current jargon is defined as 'secondary' services – that is, adult or child and adolescent mental health services. However, many will feel able and willing to talk to their GP about issues affecting their family life and seek advice, sympathy or simply a listening ear.

The GP's position

In our experience of working in general practice, both single handed and group practices, general practitioners are in principle willing to take on board a counselling role when emotional difficulties occur. However, they often do not feel equipped or trained to deal with the emotional impact that family life events have on their patients. Nevertheless, despite the limited amount of time available in the context of the consultation, GPs are increasingly eager to take more of a holistic perspective on the difficulties presented by their patients and want to understand and address the meaning of individual symptoms in the context of family relationships (Dowling, 1994).

This chapter will address ways in which GPs and other primary care professionals might attend to the distress presented to them, often through explicit physical symptoms presented by patients going through or in the aftermath of divorce. However, it must be acknowledged that whilst GPs and primary care professionals are increasingly aware of the mind–body links, the pressures and demands of an under-resourced and overstretched health service make it quite difficult for them to create adequate time and space to address the emotional side of patients' lives.

Advantages of dealing with family transitions in the context of primary care

- *Ordinariness*: Because most people have a GP who they are likely to have consulted at different stages of their life-cycle, the experience of discussing and sharing a particular family transition and the effect on members of the family will feel more 'ordinary' if it takes place in this familiar territory. The problems or difficulties will be explored in the context of an *evolutionary relationship* not in the context of being referred to a different service and therefore becoming a *different type* of patient.

  General practitioners can make links between their patients' physical symptoms and difficulties in other areas of their lives in the course of an ordinary consultation, and enable them to make changes which will have an impact on their physical as well as their mental health.
- *A developmental view*: It is possible to see the transition as part of the pattern of the family's previous management of transitions and the GP will have a view about how particular events affect particular families, so that this event can be looked at in the wider context of the family history.
- *How do families deal with loss: do they carry on 'as normal'? Are the children expected to carry on or manage on their own? How do members of the family deal with change? What support systems are available to them?* These are some of the questions the GP might ask when seeing a family going through the process of separation or divorce. The examples below illustrate how, in the context of an ordinary surgery, the GP's intervention can make a

substantial difference to patients' understanding and handling of a situation.

Mrs Long was worried about her son, Darren, aged 8. She had been called to the school and the teachers had expressed concern about his aggressive behaviour. Mrs L had also experienced Darren's aggression at home and was finding it increasingly difficult to control him. She consulted her GP because she was having headaches, especially first thing in the morning when she was trying to get ready for work and had to battle with Darren to get ready for school. The GP asked if there had been any changes at home. Mrs L explained that she and her husband had separated. It had been difficult for a long time and he had finally left. She had tried to 'carry on as normal' as she thought not talking about it would make it easier for Darren. The contact with Darren's father was erratic as he travelled a lot as part of his work. Visits were usually preceded by difficult and acrimonious telephone calls with Mrs L trying to ensure that Darren would not be let down. However, when his father did call Darren would be as good as gold with him, even if he had been waiting for hours to be collected. The GP suggested that maybe Darren felt very angry with his father but did not dare express it directly to him, in case the precarious contact would cease altogether. He thought it would be helpful to Darren to be able to talk with someone about his feelings. Mrs L felt reassured by the GP that talking with Darren would be helpful to him rather than damaging, and thought she would start by explaining the situation fully to him.

Mrs L and Darren visited the GP a few weeks later as Darren had sprained his ankle playing football. The GP enquired how things were at home and Mrs L explained openly, in front of Darren, that they had 'a good talk and got it all out of our system and were able to be upset together'. Darren had calmed down at school and had asked his dad if he would like to come and watch him play football as he was now in a football team and had to play matches on Saturdays. Dad was very proud of Darren's football achievements and was beginning to take an interest in coming to watch him at play.

In this situation, as in many others, the GP's intervention, given the relationship of trust which already existed with the family, was sufficient for things to change. Other situations are more complex and entrenched and may require longer and more intense interventions, or even a referral to other professionals either within or outside the practice.

Do family members show their grief though their bodies? Do they tend to get ill rather than being sad?

Mr T came to see his GP because he was feeling very 'run down'. He thought he had a virus. The GP asked about any changes in Mr T's life, and Mr T talked about his recent separation and his excruciating emotional pain regarding the children. He felt very clear that he saw no future for the marriage, but he found it very difficult not to see the children as often as he would like to, but was holding back as he thought it would make it easier for the children. The GP was able to explain that it would be beneficial for the children to have as much contact as possible with their father. Mr T felt reassured and the GP's opinion empowered him to re-open negotiations about contact with his wife on the basis of what was best for the children.

Levels of intervention

What can be achieved in a general consultation

The GP will be able to ask relevant questions, acknowledge the links and connections between the symptoms and the distressing aspects of the separation and divorce, and maybe enable a parent to accept that a child might be manifesting his or her distress in a particular way. Families will find it a relief to have their mixed feelings recognised and be helped to make sense of them. There will be situations when such a link cannot be made explicit, or the parent is reluctant to accept that there might be a connection.

The following are useful questions for GPs to ask when thinking about the children experiencing the separation or divorce of their parents:

- Is the child despondent, losing interest in school or extra curricular activities?
- Is the child getting ill more often, missing school, consulting for various ailments?
- Are eating patterns/habits changing significantly?

- Are they more quarrelsome or aggressive, either at home or at school?
- Are they avoiding friends, going out, mixing socially?
- Are they watchful of the parents, worrying about their physical or mental well-being.
- Are they afraid to assert their wishes in case they upset the parents (particularly the 'non-resident' parent); that is, missing activities in order to fit in with parent contact time, not going on school journeys, missing friends' parties, and so on.

A GP's checklist (especially if the parent consults about the child regarding any of the above) might include the following:

- Has the child been given an explanation of the reasons for the break up of the family?
- Is there a routine and predictable arrangements for contact with the out of house parent?
- Is there conflict/violence in the parental relationship?
- Are the parents able to communicate directly, or do they do so through the child?
- Can the parents think of the child's needs first?
- Are there new partners involved?

When to make a longer/special appointment

Some GPs find it useful to schedule a longer appointment when it becomes clear that it will not be possible to have a proper discussion as part of the ordinary surgery. This 'special appointment' will convey the message to the patient that the GP has understood the need for a proper space to explore the issue.

Ellie, aged 17, had gone to the GP because, yet again, her eczema had flared up. She was fed up about it, she said, particularly as the summer was approaching. 'Could she have a different cream? something that really works please!' Her GP had known Ellie since she was a little girl and had quite a lot of contact with her because of her recurring eczema. The GP thought Ellie looked rather tense and when she asked if everything was all right, Ellie, avoiding eye contact, muttered something about being fed up with all the arguments at home and her parents being unreasonable. The GP suggested there might be things Ellie would like to talk about, but Ellie stood up saying 'got to go, I'm going on a geography field trip'. The GP suggested Ellie came at the end of surgery the next day when they could have a bit of extra time. Ellie agreed. With adolescents, it is important not to leave too long a gap as the willingness to talk may not last. She gave her a prescription so Ellie could start treating her eczema at once. Ellie turned up the next day; she'd put the cream on and it seemed to be working. The GP did not need to say much: Ellie explained that her mum and dad were always arguing and she thought they might split up. Mum had been talking about going off to Ireland to live with her sister. Ellie was very confused and angry. She found herself thinking about it all the time and wasn't concentrating at school. She'd been going to clubs and staying out late. Once or twice she had come home drunk and had a big row with her father. Floods of tears followed but gradually she felt relieved to have talked. The GP arranged for her to see the practice counsellor. Ellie liked that idea. It would help her to sort herself out...

The role of health visitors

Health visitors are the professionals who are in touch with the families from the start of parenthood, and their role is defined by the fact that there is a new member in the family, not by any problems presented. Their role enables them to see how the patterns of relationship evolve when the baby arrives, and they are usually very aware of the support, or lack of it, available to new parents. Health visitors have access to the home environment and also see the mothers and babies at the baby clinic when parents come to have their babies weighed and to get advice about feeding, sleeping and any other developmental issues. Health visitors are in an ideal position to pick up the parents' anxieties relating to bringing up children. By virtue of their role they can also recognise the stresses and strains in the parents' relationship, and often mothers will confide in them either in the safety of their home or when they visit the clinic.

Sharon, a young mother of two children, was worried about her two-year-old daughter Katie 'playing up' and not going to sleep. She was feeling harassed as there was such a lot to do with a toddler and a baby. The baby was still waking up at night and with Katie not going to bed early Sharon wasn't getting enough sleep and felt exhausted. She came to the clinic to have the baby weighed and the health visitor, who knew her well, noticed how drained she looked and suggested a home visit later in the week. When she called, she found a tense atmosphere. Mark, Sharon's partner, was at home; he had recently been made redundant. This situation had created considerable tension in the couple's relationship and they had been rowing a lot. The health visitor was able to talk to both of them about the link between the rows and Katie's unsettled behaviour. Maybe she was anxious and got a bit frightened. They talked about strategies to manage Katie at bed time, and the health visitor asked Mark and Sharon if they would like to go for counselling. Mark flatly refused. He felt safe talking to the health visitor in the privacy of their home and thought their discussion had been really helpful. They also talked about Sharon going to the local family centre where she could get some support. A few weeks later the health visitor called again, and found a more relaxed Sharon. Katie was now getting to bed without any hassle, and after her bath Mark was reading her a story while Sharon saw to the baby. They seemed to be arguing less and Mark had been looking for jobs.

The Health Visitor's role was crucial in this situation which might well have escalated and led to the break-up of the family. Unfortunately, the increasing pressures and limited resources militate against these valuable professionals spending more time with young families. Their preventative role with families is absolutely essential and should be supported and expanded. As a report from a pilot project for the screening and treatment of women with post-natal depression states,

> Health visiting has an important role in supporting the health needs of young children and their families. To be an effective service, it is critical that children are not viewed in isolation from the adults who care for them. (Fuggle *et al.*, 1998, p. 10)

Because of the nature of their contact with families, health visitors often see or hear enough to worry about particular children. However, at times it is difficult for other professionals to listen or take sufficiently seriously their level of concern. Yet, by virtue of the decline of social services, it is not infrequent to see a health visitor agonising and being left holding all the anxiety about a family where there might be a suspicion of child sexual or physical abuse. Health visitors see and hear things which may alert other professionals to potential, if not actual, risks to children.

In the practice where one of us works, a *Primary Care Team Meeting* takes place weekly. It provides an opportunity for all the practitioners to raise their concerns about patients and get the views and support of colleagues followed by specific action if necessary. The following is an example of a health visitor raising the awareness of the primary care team:

When discussing baby Peter the team was wondering about possible developmental delay. The health visitor reported her concern about the parents. The mother spoke little English and seemed very isolated. When the health visitor visited she always found Peter either in the pram or in the play pen with lots of toys around him. However, there seemed to be little interaction with his mother. The health visitor also noticed lots of lists on the wall with schedules of when things needed to be done down to the most minor detail. When she enquired about this, Mrs M explained that her husband left all these lists and wanted to keep control of everything she did and all her movements. She felt very depressed and was thinking of leaving him. This information threw new light on the family circumstances and the possible effect on Peter's development. It was then possible to think how the team might address the family issues and support the health visitor.

The health visitor can watch for:

In the child
- Sleeping/feeding difficulties;
- restlessness;
- difficulty in settling, anxious behaviour;
- frequent crying;
- failure to thrive.

In the parent
- excessive preoccupation with their own health;
- depression;
- changes of, or unpredictable, child-care arrangements;
- new relationships taking a lot of time and energy.

Involving a mental health professional in the GP consultation: a model for a general-practice-based family consultation service

In a group practice in north London, one of the general practitioners who is also a trained family therapist suggested having someone from the Tavistock Clinic to provide an outreach/consultation service in his practice. In this practice, where one of us works, we have evolved a model of creating special space for family consultations with the GP and a clinical psychologist/family therapist. This provides an opportunity, different from the general surgery consultation, for the family to have time and space to think about specific dilemmas (Dowling, 1998).

From the beginning it was clear that it was important to provide a service to families who would come in distress to the practice but would not necessarily accept or consider a referral to a mental health service. We thought the service offered would not be 'family therapy' as practised in specialist services, but something more consonant with the context of primary care. We decided to call it Family Consultation and kept an open mind about the number of sessions we would offer the families, although we were clear we would not be engaging in long-term interventions. In fact, the average number of sessions we have offered to families has been between three and five, as in the example below.

When the family are asked to come for a family consultation in the context of the general practice, are aware of their history with their GP, and the introduction of the specialist practitioner will add a new dimension to a consultation taking place within a safe and known relationship. It becomes possible to explore the area of family relationships using the GP's knowledge which provides a kind of 'shorthand' for the connections between events in the family's life-cycle. The GP will also know the family's coping strategies at times of stress and is likely to be aware of what does and does not work for them.

On the other hand, the specialist practitioner will be able to use the position of outsider, 'not knowing', to ask questions which might introduce a different perspective to the situation and which will allow the GP to take a back-seat. For GPs, working in isolation and with enormous pressures of time and demands made on them, having another professional to work with and to reflect represents a valuable and valued resource. At the same time the GP needs to feel free to return to routine aspects of general practice without having to enquire about the troubled relationships every time.

Working with families in general practice

The P family:

The family consisted of mother and her two children aged seven and five. Mother was worried about the eldest child, Laura, who was withdrawn, particularly at school. Father had left the family several years ago and mother had felt relieved by his going as, in her view, 'he couldn't take responsibility for fatherhood'. The school had defined Laura as lacking self-esteem, and Mrs P had taken her worries to her GP who thought it would be useful to offer a family consultation.

We met with Mrs P in the first instance, as she was feeling very apprehensive about bringing her children to see the psychologist. In the context of what she experienced as a very safe relationship with the GP we were able to explore her main worries and begin to think about what the children, particularly Laura, might need. Mrs P was very anxious as Mr P has not kept up contact with the children. We learned how Mrs P has kept up the 'pretence' of father's interest by buying presents and cards for the children on their birthdays and at Christmas, and giving them as if father had sent them. The GP knew about this but had found it difficult to find a way of saying to Mrs P that this was not very helpful. We also heard from Mrs P that Laura blamed herself for daddy going and would have occasional temper tantrums which left mother feeling impotent and devastated as she felt unable to 'get through' to Laura. Mother also shared with us her anxieties about letting the children go out and her dread of the future when they may ask to go to the shops or to the park on their own.

In this context it was clear that with such fears of 'the unknown' it would not have been possible for the GP to refer the family anywhere else. However, in the familiar and safe context of her trusted GP surgery, Mrs P was able to share her worries and agreed to a family session.

We decided it would be important to begin to talk more realistically about the children's relationship (or lack of it) with their father. The GP was anxious about how mother would take this but felt confident that together we could tackle the consequences.

At the next session we were struck by the difference between Laura and Sam her younger brother. Laura came in sucking her thumb and went to hide behind mother's chair. Later in the session she climbed under the examination couch in an attempt to avoid eye contact. She responded to the GP's attempts to make contact with her but did not utter a word. Sam, on the other hand, felt compelled to 'fill up' the session being very animated, giggling and talking all the time. We agreed we needed to talk about daddy and I suggested that at times it might seem to the children as if daddy was not interested in them. Maybe that made them feel angry, particularly Laura, and maybe Sam thought he had to be busy and active all the time to keep these unpleasant thoughts out of his mind. At that point mother whispered to the GP *'I don't like the idea of telling them their dad doesn't care about them'*. We understood that it was difficult to continue talking about this but the children seemed thoughtful and somewhat relieved after the intervention. We suggested Mrs P discussed with Mr P possible arrangements for contact, stressing the fact that the children loved him and would like to see him.

At a follow-up consultation we heard the children were now seeing their father regularly and Laura was more talkative at school. However, there were inappropriate roles she was holding as 'go-between' for the parents. We were able to talk about the strain put on Laura by having to negotiate contact visits and make decisions which more appropriately should be made by her parents. At the end of the consultation we heard that Laura and Sam were gradually being allowed a bit more independence without mother feeling too anxious about it. We decided it would be appropriate at that point to terminate the family sessions and for the GP to hear if there were any further worries which would warrant further joint work.

Discussion after the session revealed how the GP had felt it had been a useful intervention and the new context had made it possible to explore different issues with the family whilst in the safe familiar context of the practice.

Working with the health visitors

One of the health visitors was worried about Jane who was very depressed. Jane had three young children and was, in the health visitor's view, expecting too much of Martin, the oldest child, aged six. Jane's demands on Martin had increased since she had separated from her husband, and she had subsequently become depressed.

In discussion with the health visitor we decided it would be best for both of us to see Jane and her children together. Jane was apprehensive about meeting someone she did not know, but she was prepared to accept the suggestion of the health visitor who she trusted.

Jane only brought the baby to the meeting, as she did not want Martin or his sister to miss school. We considered this appropriate, and it soon became apparent that Jane had done a lot of thinking and wanted to make sense, helped by us, of what was going on between her and Martin. As the oldest child in her family of origin, Jane had had a lot of demands placed on her by her mother in relation to looking after her younger brothers and sisters. She had grown up without a father and was very aware of what Martin was missing, but somehow could not help placing demands on him. It was all she knew, 'for kids to help parents out when they can't cope!' She had talked to the health visitor before about her early experiences, and therefore it felt safe, as it were, to continue the conversation. We moved on to explore what might make it possible for Jane to free Martin from age-inappropriate responsibilities and avail herself of other support systems. Jane would like to be able to have more social contact with other parents but felt anxious about joining any group. We thought together how this might be possible and the health visitor suggested going with her to the local mother and toddler group. This appealed to Jane. We also thought of the possibility of the two older children going to an after-school play centre for a couple of days a week in order to give Jane a bit of space. We then talked about the developmental needs of the children, particularly Martin. Despite being the oldest, he was only six, and needed play and stimulation rather than fetching and carrying for mother all the time. A few weeks later on a follow-up visit, the health visitor heard Jane had made a couple of friends at the mother and toddler group and was enjoying going. The children were happy at the play centre and Jane was more able to think of Martin as a child in his own right rather than as a 'little man' as she put it.

The value of consultation

Gradually the role has extended to different levels of work in the practice to include:

- Work with the other GPs, which involves seeing families together as well as discussing cases which are worrying to them.
- Consultancy to the GPs as a group around issues involving the organisation and running of the practice. In the midst of

the pressures of working in general practice, having an out-side professional to think with them about their work can help to ensure that adequate time and space is safeguarded to reflect on the nature of the work, the relationships between members of the practice and dilemmas arising from the work with patients and staff.

- Working with members of the primary care team. This involves space to discuss concerns with the practice nurses or health visitors, or seeing families together with them as in the case of Jane and Martin.

The practice counsellor/therapist

With the shift towards comprehensive services in primary care, the role of the practice counsellor becomes increasingly import-ant. Practitioners with a background in individual or family ther-apy can provide a useful service in the context of the practice, which makes it more accessible and less daunting for patients than a referral to specialist services. Whatever their model of practice, a family evaluation which takes into account the impact of family relationships on the individual is particularly helpful. It is worth emphasising that ongoing communication with the gen-eral practitioners about the psychological work done in the prac-tice is the best way to ensure that the patients and their families are adequately held in mind.

For some years, clinical psychologists have worked in the context of primary care (Deys, Dowling and Golding, 1989) and increasingly their role has shifted from taking referrals to a more consultative approach. Likewise, in recent years family therapists and counsellors have been employed by practices wishing to develop more integrated services. When working with individuals or fam-ilies going through the divorce process these professionals can provide valuable help in the safe context of the family's general practice. The following are some issues which professionals in pri-mary care may need to help parents to think about when going through separation and divorce:

- Parents most probably will not agree in their own version of the events leading up to the separation, but it is important that they are helped to agree on key points to tell the children.

- *Who should tell them?* If possible, parents should talk to the children together, but if this is not an option the agreed points will help the children have a coherent explanation.
- *How will children's lives change*: It is very useful for parents to explain to their children the specific ways in which their lives might change.
- *Distinction between the couple splitting up and parents remaining parents, though in different circumstances*: Helping parents make this distinction explicit to the children helps them to evolve a new story about their family which will include the loss of the family as it was, but will enable them to move on to a different kind of relationship with each parent as explained in Chapters 4 and 5.

In this chapter we have addressed some of the ways in which practitioners can help families through the process of separation and divorce. The advantages of the primary care context, as a safe environment in which families can address these issues, and specific signals to watch for in children have been outlined.

Summary

When dealing with separation and divorce, practitioners in primary care need to pay attention to:

- The ways families deal with loss and change.
- The support systems available to families.
- The ways family members may show their grief through their bodies.
- Problematic behaviour exhibited by children either at home or at school.
- Increasing frequency of illness in the family.
- Changes in the family structure such as new partners and/or new stepsiblings.
- Changes affecting the children, in particular contact with the non-resident parent, or changes in living arrangements.

10

BROADENING THE CONTEXT: APPLICATIONS IN DIFFERENT PROFESSIONAL CONTEXTS

Throughout this book we have examined the conditions under which children may be particularly vulnerable, and we have looked at the risks as well as the protective factors that will promote resilience in children and families. Our work has been done in the context of a multidisciplinary Child and Family Mental Health Service. In this chapter we consider how a range of professionals who are likely to come into contact with children going through the family transitions following separation and divorce can bear in mind the dilemmas we have described as these relate to their own work. We have focused in particular on those who are likely to work directly with children as they go through divorce and family change. We are aware of the many other professionals whose contact with the family or focus of work may be different, who will nonetheless be working with children for whom divorce and family reordering is a large part of their childhood experience. The problems for which they are referred may not be directly connected to separation issues by the referring person. However, it is important for professionals to bear these issues in mind and to ask about them when considering what help to offer. Similarly, professionals working with adults, particularly in the social services and mental health field, will need to remember the relevance of divorce to their clients' experience, or to the experience of their clients' children.

Research and clinical experience

From research and clinical experience we know that children do better if:

- There is no ongoing conflict between the parents.
- They maintain free and easy contact with both parents.
- They have a coherent explanation about the break-up of the family.
- They have stability and predictability in terms of contact arrangements with the out-of-house parent.
- They have reliable support systems outside the family.
- They have a supportive school environment, sensitive to their needs and family circumstances.
- Neither of their parents suffers mental health problems.

Professionals working directly with children

As children develop they come into contact with a number of professionals who will be involved with them either because they are concerned and responsible for a particular stage of development, or because there are specific issues bringing a particular child to their attention. Any of these professionals may have the opportunity to have a conversation with a child who has experienced the separation or divorce of their parents. In this chapter we outline some guiding principles and give examples of what we found helpful in our clinical work with children.

The following diagram represents the different professional systems children may relate to in the course of their development:

Health system
Primary care:
  general practitioners
  health visitors, school nurses
  school doctors

Specialists services:
  child development team psychiatrists
  psychologists
  psychotherapists, paediatrician
  other child health specialists
  adult mental health practitioners

Education
Teachers, special-needs coordinators
education social workers
educational psychologists
learning support services

Social services
who should be bearing children in
  mind on behalf of parents.

CHILD AND FAMILY

Legal
Solicitors/barristers
judge
court welfare officer
guardian ad litem
official solicitor

Resources available in the community
Extended family, social network
place of worship, neighbourhood clubs
societies, child care system/child
  minders
playgroup, nurseries

The health context

Children and their families come into contact with general practitioners and health visitors throughout their development as described in Chapter 9. School nurses and doctors also have a role to play in relation to assessing their physical development and detecting any causes for concern. However, if there are specific problems in terms of their health, learning or behaviour, or if they have special physical, emotional or educational needs, they may attend a child development team or a specialist clinic.

Child and family mental health teams

Children can be referred to a Child and Family Mental Health Service where they may be seen by one or more members of the multidisciplinary team: a clinical psychologist, a child psychiatrist, a child psychotherapist, a family therapist or a social worker. Any of these mental health professionals may be involved in the assessment and therapeutic intervention, and may see children on their own as well as with the family. They may also be required to prepare court reports as expert witnesses, or to advise the court on children's needs, parental contact and parents' capacity to parent.

Any of these professionals may come into contact with lone-parent families, stepfamilies or families going through the process of separation and divorce as part of their service delivery. Children will be referred either because they are presenting emotional or behavioural difficulties, or because the parents or referring agency make a connection between their difficulties and the separation or divorce of their parents. As explained in Chapters 3, 4 and 5, we have developed a model which we hope can be adapted and implemented in other child and family mental health settings. We have evolved the following guiding principles :

1. Provide a therapeutic setting which will be a secure base from which to explore different ways of relating in a new family context.
2. In order to hear the different 'voices', particularly the children's, it is useful to combine individual and family interviews.
3. Enable each parent to give their side of the 'story' but keep the focus firmly on working towards cooperative parenting.

4. Provide an opportunity for children to express their views and feelings and help them communicate their anxieties and hopes to their parents.
5. Discuss specific contact arrangements with both parents.
6. A focus on the management of conflict rather than searching for motives or reasons is especially important for long-term contact disputes.

Specific issues for psychotherapists and counsellors

- *Child psychotherapists* are specially trained to understand the inner world of children. Increasingly, they work within the context of the children's relationships with the family and others who may be looking after them, and take account of changes in the outer reality of a child's existence. Awareness of some of the powerful and sustained conflicts that can form a daily part of the child's external reality in the context of divorce is likely to make a child psychotherapist better placed to help parents, as well as other professionals working with the family, to keep the child's views and needs in mind.
- *Adult psychotherapists and counsellors* who are working with patients in the context of a stressful divorce may also need to bear in mind the effects of these processes on the children involved. The degree to which a therapist actively enquires into the lives of their patients will remain a matter of difference between schools of psychotherapy. We would like to draw attention to the importance of promoting a warm and continuous parenting function on behalf of the patient's children. An awareness of the impact of family relationships on the individual is particularly useful to those working in adult mental health.
- *Family Therapists* normally take the family as the primary unit of their work, also looking at the wider social network with which different members are involved and relating to this where the family, or the therapist, think it would be useful. The focus is on the relationships between different members and the interactions and communications between them. It became apparent early in our own clinical work with families in transition that it was very difficult for children's voices to be heard, and for the different perspective of children on the processes

taking place in the family to be taken into account in parental planning about some of the small details of their lives. It also became evident that children were often in a loyalty bind between their parents, and the different stories that they told about the separation and divorce. This made it difficult for children to talk about their own stress and concerns arising from the experience of parental separation while they were in the presence of one or both parents.

Current family therapy theory emphasises a way of looking at family process that picks out dominant and submerged discourses in families (Gorell Barnes, 1998; Gorell Barnes and Dowling, 1997), and this awareness has been key to the way our own work developed, as described in Chapters 2, 3 and 5. We suggest that family therapists should take into account how difficult it is for children to get a hearing at times when there is a conflict of interest between them and their parents over how their future lives are to be lived. Paying attention to the children's perspective leads to changes in the way that arrangements may subsequently be made, and some of the sense of powerlessness accompanying a parental decision to split up can be alleviated in relation to the planning of their daily lives.

The school context

During the pre-school and school years, nursery staff and teachers become a crucial influence as described in Chapters 2 and 8. *Special-needs coordinators* as well as *educational psychologists* and *education social workers* may become involved in relation to educational problems. One of the main tasks of educational psychologists is to assess children with special educational needs, and their assessment is a major contributing factor to the decision relating to special educational provision for children. It is very important that, as part of their assessment they ascertain the family context and any factors related to family relationships which may be affecting children's performance at school. In the same way, these factors may affect children's performance on psychometric tests and the written report must reflect this. The results of cognitive standardised tests must be interpreted with caution and explicit reference must be made to the family circumstances that may be affecting children's intellectual functioning.

Educational psychologists have an important role to play as consultants to schools and in providing in-service training for teachers. They can help teachers to consider the relationship between the family and the school and enable them to develop and implement ideas which will help children and their families through this transition. Blacher (1997), in a small study investigating the views of five educational psychologists and five teachers about their role in relation to divorce, found that the educational psychologists identified a lack of fit between schools' priorities and their own beliefs about their role. They saw schools as primarily interested in their service in relation to individual case work and assessment, while they saw their role as being able to bring a different perspective at a consultative level and through in-service training in relation to issues of separation and divorce and their effects on pupils. All teachers interviewed felt that educational psychologists might have a role to play, supporting teachers with their expert knowledge and through training, but felt their role was restricted by time constraints and the apparent priority for statutory assessment.

Education social workers work at the interface between home and school and will have opportunities to explore changes in family circumstances and their effect on children's adjustment at school.

Children, divorce and the legal context

At the time of separation and divorce, solicitors and the court system may become involved and children may be interviewed by court welfare officers and guardians ad litem, who will have the task of assessing their wishes and understanding and making recommendations to the courts regarding what is best for the children's future. A number of stages at which parents and professionals may jointly consider children's future interests punctuates the divorce process.

All parties will, under the new divorce law (The Family Law Act 1996) be expected to attend an information meeting. Under section 8(9) whoever conducts such meetings will be expected to provide information on a number of matters relating to separation and divorce, but in three ways that relate in particular to issues of children:

- The importance to be attached to the welfare, wishes and feelings of children.
- How the parties may acquire a better understanding of the ways in which children can be helped to cope with the breakdown of a marriage.
- Protection available against violence, and how to obtain support and assistance.

Children will also be looked out for under section 11(4) where the concept of the welfare of the child as 'paramount' is spelled out in particular detail relating to the 'child's voice'. Under Section 11(4), in treating the welfare of the child as paramount the court is directed to have particular regard to:

- The wishes and feelings of the child considered in the light of his or her age and understanding, and the circumstances in which those wishes were expressed.
- The conduct of the parties in relation to the upbringing of the child.
- The general principle that in the absence of evidence to the contrary the welfare of the child will be best served by:

    1. the child having regular contact with those who have parental responsibility for him or her and with other members of his or her family; and
    2. the maintenance of as good a continuing relationship with his or her parents as is possible.

Risk to the child concerns details about place and persons with whom the child might subsequently have contact:

- The place where the person with whom the child will reside is living or proposes to live.
- Any person with whom that person is living or with whom he or she proposes to live.
- Any other arrangements for his or her care and upbringing.

Section 11(4) imposes a duty on the court 'on the evidence before it' to consider *inter alia* the wishes and feeling of the child and the conduct of the parties in relation to the upbringing of the child. In Chapter 4 we have illustrated the complexities involved in making a true assessment of the conduct of parents, and in Chapter 5 the difficulties that children may have in expressing their own wishes and feelings. Whereas the implementation of separate representation for children under section 64 in Part 5 of the act might well achieve a difference in how children's views are taken into account, the resource implications are enormous. A recent analysis of the Family Law Bill (Bailey-Harris, 1997) suggests that

> the philosophy of private ordering and non-intervention in the relationship between children and parents other than in exceptional circumstances is not compatible with the ascertainment of children's wishes and feelings by those other than the parents as a general rule. Experts in child care law doubt whether there will be sufficient funding for children in private law proceedings to be represented by a guardian ad litem. (p. 13)

In view of the particular expertise of professionals attached to the courts in working with children we would expect our own experience to have both replications and differences from work undertaken in a legal framework. However, the principles of working with children laid out below, and the work with fathers as well as mothers described elsewhere in the book, may well be complementary to much that is already done. We hope that it may open up further dialogues between professionals from different backgrounds.

The role of mediators

Robinson (1997) provides a succinct and useful account for other professionals of the legal aspects of separation which have to be negotiated as part of the divorce process. In her description of the work of mediators it is possible to see both the differences of emphasis and the similarities of style to work undertaken in the context of problems presenting through the referral of children for help with disturbed behaviour:

1. Establishing the forum – the mediator outlines the process to the couple who can then choose whether to take part, sometimes, particularly when mediating on all issues (issues to do with finance as well as to do with the children), signing an agreement to engage in the process.
2. Clarifying the issues – the mediator explores the present situation with the couple, making an explicit note of the areas on which they disagree, and outlines an agenda which they clarify; they then begin to look at the order in which these may be approached.
3. Exploring the issues – the mediator takes charge of the process, carefully maintaining impartiality between the couple throughout. The mediator does not recommend solutions, and s/he carefully manages the differences, employing various techniques.
4. Developing the options – this is the process of negotiation, in which the couple is helped with floating and testing ideas in the confidential safety of the mediation process.
5. Securing agreement – the mediator, with the agreement of the couple, draws up a memorandum of understanding which they agree to take to their respective lawyers for legal advice. (*Ibid.*, p. 53)

Robinson points out some of the difficulties that have been found in the country as a whole in including children in the mediation process. A major aim in mediation is to reach agreement regarding property, finance and the children, and only secondarily for there to be a therapeutic spin-off. A national family mediation working party report found that 'when children were directly involved many mediators, by seeing the children, opted out of the mediation process, opting in again subsequently' (*Ibid.*, p. 59).

From our own experience, we would suggest that children become a complicating factor in a mediation process because:

1. They bring their own distress to the situation.
2. They highlight the conflict of interests between parents and children in a crude sense – it is not which parent a child may want to go with but the fact that children do not want parents to divorce.

3. They are likely to take the family in the general direction of a therapeutic interview by raising questions beyond the boundaries of the mediation guidelines.

While therapeutic work does not have to become a long process, it may well involve aspects of family pain, grief and general ways of behaving which are not yet within the brief or the 'training repertoires' of some mediators. Robinson outlines the principles of divorce-related intervention with children in mediation at the Institute of Family Therapy (London), and the approach she describes goes some way towards incorporating both the stricter boundaries of a mediation approach with the values of having the child's voice heard in the mediation process. Because we were seeing children who had already taken on board the parental divorce and were showing related problems through their behaviour, the processes we describe in this book do not always fit within a tightly defined framework, although we could equally argue, with hindsight, that a tight framework was especially useful in some long-standing dispute cases around aspects of the child's post-divorce care.

Questions of what sort of help can be offered to children during these stressful times remain wide open with much room for mediators and family therapists to discuss and refine their ideas further (given time and space to do so) As Robinson points out, the recommendation by the consortium of children's charities failed in their proposal that the bill should allow the Lord Chancellor to make regulations for a 'special children's officer attached to family court centres who would act as a reference and co-ordination point for parents and children wanting information, consultation and if necessary representation for children' (Robinson, 1997, p. 61). The field is therefore still wide open for each and all professionals to act within this framework as appropriate to their professional position in regard to the child's life.

Social work, divorce, domestic violence and child protection

Stanley (1997) has reviewed the issues relating to child protection and social work practice in the context of domestic violence and child abuse. It is in this area that social workers are most likely to practice directly with children and their parents in the post-divorce context. She draws attention to the difficulties besetting social workers which include practitioners' fears of challenging violent men and problems of cultural relativism, in which both class and culture can be misused to legitimate male violence to women and children. A major difficulty is female workers' own sense of ineffectiveness in helping women and children who are living in ongoing situations of abuse.

Two contributions from our work may be relevant to social work practice and training. Firstly an emphasis on working with fathers as well as mothers, and secondly the value of combining individual and family interviewing. Stanley highlights the general experience of how male intimidation can threaten women professionals as well as women clients. She points out how a shift from offering services currently focused on women and children, to services which would include intervention with abusing men, carries significant resource and training implications for social work. Currently work with men who abuse is mainly carried out within the probation service, and conviction in a court of law creates the precondition for treatment.

The subject of working with men who are violent is too large for us to address within the framework of this book (see Chapter 6). However, our own experience co-working as child-oriented professionals suggests a different way forward which supports the need for additional resources. We highlight three key aspects:

1. A safe context for doing the work.
2. A parenting-oriented approach with men.
3. An opportunity for the men and the women to tell their own story separately.

In combining these three points in our approach we observed that a safe context for doing the work protects both the violent man and the woman professional side by side. A man who hits his partner and/or his children may need an opportunity to broaden his own experience of himself. His definitions of himself can be expanded by placing his violent behaviour in a wider context of his own life story, as well as in the context of his positive wishes to father his children in better ways than he was fathered himself. Conversations which touch on painful feelings, guilt and shame, as well as challenging violent behaviours require a safe setting. As the violent impulses are experienced, the knowledge that they cannot be acted on allows the thinking to move forward to other ways in which such feelings might be named and handled in the context of the family. Bringing in the additional voice of a colleague speaking on behalf of the child emphasises the opportunity for a man to grow through the experience of parenting. In addition, *an educative stance towards what children need from their parents and how this may be done, keeps the focus on the reality of what is possible.*

In this chapter we have explored the application of our work to different professional settings. The book is not intended to be prescriptive, and we hope that readers will take what they can use in their own context. We have tried to distil some principles for practice. In our teaching and consultation we have recognised the difficulties that many adults have in eliciting the views of children around painful issues. Below we outline some of the techniques we have found helpful in our therapeutic work.

Interviewing children

As explained in Chapter 5, the conditions for a child to feel safe in the presence of any of these professionals, have to be created for them to feel free to talk about their thoughts and feelings. As most professionals know, it is usually necessary to see children with their parents or carers in the first instance and fully explain the purpose of the individual interview if the children are going to be seen on their own. With all children, but especially with younger ones, it is important to make sure that they know exactly how long the interview will last, where the parent or carer will be, and how children can contact them should they become distressed. A brief statement clarifying these points will reassure the child of the boundaries around the particular session and will help them deal with some of the anxieties about being interviewed on their own.

In order to avoid putting children in a loyalty bind by asking questions which would need them to express a preference for one parent over the other, specific questions can be asked about life with each parent:

- *'What is good about being with dad (or mum)?'* will elicit the experiences children may find positive. On the other hand, responses such as 'we can go to bed when we like', 'we can watch videos till late', or 'we always have take-away', will throw light on what kind of boundaries or what level of care the children might be getting.

Danny, aged 13, whose father is an artist, talked with delight about going to different places with dad, but closer questioning revealed a fairly chaotic schedule, which didn't enable Danny to go to bed at a regular time, nor did it leave much time to do homework. The school had been complaining about him looking very tired and lacking in concentration. In Danny's situation he much preferred his time with Dad as he did not get on with his stepfather, but it was necessary to discuss with his father what changes he could make in his lifestyle in order to provide Danny with an age-appropriate schedule which was conducive to his doing well at school.

- *'What is different about being with dad now he doesn't live with you?'* Such a question will enable children to reflect on the differences that have affected their lives and what the effects have been on them. Do they have a quiet place to do homework? Do they have to travel far to school? Can they have friends round? With parents who are mentally or physically ill the children may be performing inappropriate tasks and becoming carers of their parents at the expense of their own emotional and social development, as described in Chapter 6.

Children need to understand that the information obtained in the interview will be used with the parents *in order to make their life better.* This may cause initial anxiety and the professional concerned will have to fully explain that they are acting on the children's behalf. But usually, in our experience, most children feel relieved that a responsible adult is going to help them voice their worries, or do it on their behalf, until they feel ready to do it themselves.

Indirect means of accessing children's thoughts and feelings

Drawings

Whether interviewing a child on their own or within the family context, many professionals find it useful to suggest that the children may do some drawing. The use of drawing will have different purposes depending on the context in which it takes place. In the context of family therapy sessions at the clinic, we have used drawings to translate the children's thoughts and feelings to the family. Children's preoccupations are often revealed in a pictorial way when they find it difficult to put them into words.

Mary, aged nine, and Craig, aged seven, were drawing during a family session where their mother was describing her anxieties about their children's contact visits to their father. She was concerned about his drug-abusing, particularly when he injected and became aggressive. Mary, who is very close to her father, was drawing a garden and a girl her age watering it. She paused from time to time to reassure her mother that it was 'really OK at dad's, don't worry I can handle it'. She clearly was listening very carefully to her mother's story and wanted to reassure her that all would be well. Later on in the session, mother complained about Mary's aggression towards her. Much to her distress she described how Mary was using foul language and on one occasion had even thrown an object at her. The drawings helped us discuss with the family Mary's experience of having to be responsible for 'keeping things nice and OK' just like the little girl with the watering can. But we could also think about another side of Mary, fragile and vulnerable, who expressed her aggression against her mum, but who also might feel frightened about what aggression does, but was not free to express her fears as she felt she had to preserve her relationship with her father. As a result of the conversation it was possible for Mary's mother to see the fragile and frightened side of a nine-year-old, not just the aggressive monster she had become in mother's mind.

Craig, on the other hand, drew a little boy in a sea full of sharks, and when asked what would happen to the little boy in the picture, he said

'He will get gobbled up by them, they are stronger and faster'. His drawing and story helped us understand his experience of feeling unsafe.

Drawings can be used to facilitate the expression of the child's feelings; however, caution must be applied to the interpretation of their meaning and any comments made to the child about them need to be put as a possibility rather than as a fact. The purpose is to assist the child in telling the story of their picture without preempting their freedom to convey the meaning of their own story. Neutral, rather than leading questions in relation to the drawings will enable the child to elaborate on what it means for them. Asking children to tell what is happening in the drawing and who the characters are will enable the child to create their own story about the drawing. Leading questions such as 'are these your brothers and sisters?' should be avoided. Drawings will have a symbolic meaning which may or may not be be decoded depending on the context in which the drawing is taking place and the experience and confidence of the professionals. Drawings are not necessarily a concrete representation of children's reality.

Play materials

Play materials may be used to facilitate communication with children. We use dolls and farm animals which help children depict situations which can reveal their preoccupations. Expression of aggression, lack of care, negative interactions expressed through play with these small objects will provide clues as to what is going on in the child's mind. Likewise, positive caring attitudes, people or animals taking care or rescuing each other can be indications of the kind of experiences the child may have or long for.

However, it is not always useful to feed our impressions back to the child. What is important is to *try and understand the meaning of play in order to make sense of the children's behaviour.*

Story telling

Children sometimes find it easier to talk at 'one remove'. Telling stories, or using puppets to tell a story, can be a useful way of establishing a rapport with a child. Puppets can provide an interactive context which helps engage the children. Again, it is important to maintain a neutral stance in order not to influence the child's version of the simulated situation. Christian, aged 10, used to bring a collection of little 'monsters' to the sessions and most of their interactions consisted of some of the monsters threatening the others who were very frightened by the threats. This recurrent theme helped us understand the connection between Christian's bullish behaviour in the playground, and the vulnerable part of him who was very scared of his father.

Projective techniques

A particular technique for eliciting stories is the use of Projective Tests. This requires specialist training and can only be used by psychologists, but they can provide useful information about the child's inner world for other professionals. These tests have been standardised and have detailed norms for the interpretation of the responses, and clinical and educational psychologists are trained to use the projective test as part of their specialists skills in psychometric assessment. Projective techniques are based on the principle of apperception, that is the capacity to selectively perceive material from the stimuli. Through the mechanism of projection, qualities, feelings and fears are 'projected' onto the standardised stimuli. It then becomes possible to compare and contrast responses using the interpreting guidelines (Dowling, in preparation).

Impact on the worker

An important aspect of the work with children is in paying attention and making sense of the impact their communications have on us. Irritating, attention-seeking, provoking, or aggressive behaviour can be extremely stressful to manage and tolerate and the impact on the worker must not be underestimated. However, trying to make sense of it in interactional terms and seeing behaviour as a communication that needs to be understood can be extremely helpful. It is essential, therefore, to create opportunities for debriefing, supervision or peer-consultation in order to address the emotional impact of the work on the worker.

Appendix: notes for parents

We would like to offer some ideas on advice to parents which different professionals may wish to use in different ways. These have been written in such a way that they can be handed to parents if it seems appropriate. A videotape for parents, 'You are both still my parents', is available (Gorell Barnes with Prestige Health Productions, 1997). Some of the things that we think are important for parents to bear in mind for their children during times of separation and change are as follows:

Telling the children

- If it is possible tell your children together. This may need a bit of rehearsal, but it is worth it. Try and reach an agreed story about what you are going to say, and keep blame and anger out of it as much as possible. However much you practise, it is likely to be an emotional event when the time comes. Leave time to talk and to have a meal together afterwards, a familiar pizza or baked beans can be very reassuring. Let them know that although one of you is leaving the house you will both still be there for them. Try to keep any raised voices out of the event. Giving the message you can still talk to them together even if you are not living together can be important.

- Be prepared to answer your children's questions, but do not feel that you have to give them private details about your relationship and what has gone wrong. If you can't answer any questions say so, rather than creating a great mystery about it which they will worry about later.

- Don't give your child impossible decisions to make like who they want to live with. The adults need to be very clear about what is realistic before they turn it into an issue of choice and loyalty for the children to begin to worry over.

- Explain to the children that it is mum and dad, the parents, who have separated; and not the parent who has separated from the children. Even if a parent has left home he or she has left because they no longer wished to live with their former husband or wife, not because they do not wish to live with the children.

- Children may need reassuring that the parent who stays in the household will not leave also. Let them know that this will not happen and tell them that they are both loved and will be looked after.

- Where it is left to one of you to tell the children, tell the child, if it is known, that the parent who is no longer in the household will continue to be their parent and will continue to see them on a regular basis. However, where this is not known it is better not to set up false promises but to undertake to find out and sort out the question of visits on behalf of the child.

- Where possible let the child know that it is alright for them to love and to miss the parent who is no longer in the household. Sad feelings and angry feelings are OK. You can let your children know that you have sad and angry feelings too without overwhelming them.
- Let your child know that it is not their fault that one of you has decided to leave or that the parents have together decided to separate. Children of all ages believe they are to blame when their parents quarrel, and when they separate this can be a confirmation of their worst fears. They will need to hear this many times. You will need to find some explanation that makes sense to you and to them over time and you may need to do some work with your partner on what story you do tell them so that they are not getting conflicting messages from each of you.
- If the children go on feeling responsible for the break-up, they may take on the job of getting you back together. It is important to watch out for this, and keep reminding them that it is not their responsibility.
- Do not create false expectations that you may get back together in an attempt to protect them from being hurt. It is best for children to have a realistic and honest perspective of the situation.

Longer-term issues

- If you are angry with your children do not tell them that they are like the parent who has gone. It is easy to use words like 'you're just like your father' when the child is doing something that reminds you of your former partner. It may make them more anxious to know you are criticising them for something that they know led to a separation.
- Try and find a regular time of day when you can have some quiet time with your children, or even with each child individually. This can be difficult when you have to reorganise so many things yourself, but it is of real value to your child.
- Encourage your child to talk about how they feel, to you, to a friend or to a grandparent or aunt or uncle that they trust. Let them know that putting feelings into words can help in the long run.
- Try to keep the number of other changes in their lives to a minimum. At a time when a child is dealing with a major change and loss in their lives, the loss of quite small things can bring out a disproportionate amount of grief.

School

- School becomes a very important place at a time when other things are shifting at home. Let the teacher know what is going on so that he or she can be in tune with emotional or moody behaviours, or with any unusual difficulties in learning. Even if you have to move home, try and keep your child at the same school so that they do not lose their friends.If you do have to move school and home, then talk to your child about which of their friends they would like to stay in touch with and how you might go about arranging this.
- Children often wish that parents could go on coming to school events together. If you find this too difficult let your child know that you just can't manage it at the moment, but that it may become easier in the future.
- Be sensitive to attending school events or other special events with a new partner. Children would often rather a parent went on their own if they can't get on with the other parent. When you do decide to make this move to go with a new partner, talk about it with your child first and get their views. It is their event after all.

Relationship with ex-partner

- Try and set up arrangements for contact that are reliable and regular. Understand how much a child looks forward to their other parent's visits and try to make sure they are not let down at the last minute. Encourage your ex-partner to try and be on time for arrangements that have been made.
- If you do disappoint your child, or you can see that they are hurt or angry, let them tell you what they feel about it. Don't just brush it under the carpet.
- If you are living out of the house, always make another date when you have finished the time you are spending together so that your child knows when they can see you again. Remember that you can keep in touch on the phone and send cards if you have to work a long way away. Let the children know when they can phone you and be there for the call. Even a personal message on an answerphone can mean a lot when you are wanting to make contact with someone very much.
- *Do not* involve your children as 'go-betweens' or message carriers.
- *Do not* use them to spy on your ex-partner or on any new relationships they may be having. It is not good for them or for you.
- *Do not* speak badly of your ex-partner in front of the children. Remember that although he or she is your 'ex', they remain the

child's parent for life. It is sometimes tempting to do so, specially when you are feeling hurt or angry, but it is really important at these times to hold on and find a moment to phone a relative or friend to get it off your chest, rather than hurt your child.

- Try not to compete with your child's 'other' parent over who loves them more. Specially beware of bidding for love through giving presents or promising treats that will make you more appealing than the other parent. If you find that the parent who is not living at home always feels they have to come with a present, try and find a way of talking to them about this.

New partners

- Meeting a new boyfriend or girlfriend is usually very uncomfortable for a child, and it is always better to talk a little bit about the new person with them beforehand. Try not to rush them into a meeting.
- Let them know something of your feelings that this is someone who is good for you. Don't expect them to rush into liking your partner, and remember that they may still be feeling loyal to their own mum or dad for many years to come. If you can let them know that you know that, and don't expect them to rush into liking your friend, this will help them to be less tangled up about it.
- Reassure them that the fact you have a new friend does not mean that you love them, your child, any less. Children often get confused about being replaced by a new partner. Reassure them that as your child they have a special place in your life which is not replaceable.
- Don't forget you and your new partner may have very different ideas about how to bring children up. Spend some time checking these out so that children don't get muddled by different sets of ideas coming from each of you.
- Be sensitive to how they take on board new stepbrothers or sisters, and give time to overseeing and talking about how these new relationships are going.

REFERENCES

Adams, J. (1996) 'Lone Fatherhood', *Practice*, Vol. 8, no. 1, pp. 15–26.

Ahrons, C.R. and Miller, R.B. (1993) 'The Effect of the Post Divorce Relationship on Paternal Involvement: A Longitudinal Analysis', *American Journal of Orthopsychiatry*, Vol. 63, pp. 441–50.

Allen, K.R. (1993) 'The Dispassionate Discourse of Children's Adjustment to Divorce', *Journal of Marriage and the Family*, Vol. 55, pp. 46–9.

Amato, P.R. and Keith, B. (1991) 'Parental Divorce and Adult Well-being; A Meta-analysis', *Journal of Marriage and the Family*, Vol. 53, pp. 43–58.

Amato, P.R. and Keith, B. (1993) 'Parental Divorce and the Well-being of the Children. A Meta-analysis', *Psychological Bulletin*, Vol. 110, pp. 26–46.

Amato, P.R. and Rezac, S.J. (1994) 'Contact with Nonresident Parents, Interparental Conflict and Children's Behaviour', *Journal of Family Issues*, Vol. 15, pp. 191–207.

Arditti, J.A. and Allen, K.R. (1993) 'Understanding Distressed Fathers' Perceptions of Legal and Relational Inequities Post-divorce', *Family and Conciliation Courts Review*, Vol. 31, pp. 461–76.

Ayalon, O. and Flasher, A. (1993) *Chain Reaction, Children and Divorce* (London: Jessica Kingsley).

Bailey-Harris, R. (1997) *The Family Lawyer's Handbook* (London: The Law Society Publications).

Bender, W.N. (1994) 'Joint Custody: The Option of Choice', *Journal of Divorce and Re-marriage*, Vol. 1, pp. 115–131.

Blacher, D. (1997) *'Divorce and the School – Teachers' and Educational Psychologists' Beliefs and Practices Surrounding the Area of Separation and Divorce'*, MSc dissertation, London, Tavistock Clinic/Brunel University.

Blacklock, N. (1998) *The Domestic Violence Intervention Project* (London: Fulham and Hammersmith).

Block, J.K., Block, J. and Gjerde, P.F. (1986) 'The Personality of Children Prior to Divorce: A Prospective Study', *Child Development*, Vol. 57, pp. 827–40.

Bowlby, J. (1977) 'The Making and Breaking of Affectional Bonds', *British Journal of Psychiatry*, Vol. 130, pp. 201–10, 421–31.

Bowlby, J. (1988) *A Secure Base: Clinical Applications of Attachment Theory* (London: Routledge).

Bradshaw, J. and Millar, J. (1991) 'Lone Parent Families in the UK', Department of Social Security Report no. 6 (London: HMSO).

Brand, E., Clingempeel, W. and Bowen-Woodward, K. (1998) 'Family Relationships and Children's Psychological Adjustment in Stepmother and Stepfather Families', in E.M. Hetherington and J.D. Arasteh (eds), *Impact of Divorce, Single Parenting and Stepparenting on Children* (New Jersey: Laurence Erlbaum Associates).

Bratley, M. (1995) *'Parents' Views of a Contact Centre'*, MSc dissertation, London, Tavistock Clinic/Brunel University.

Burghes, L. (1994) 'Lone Parenthood and Family Disruption', Occasional Paper no. 18 (London: Family Policy Studies Centre).

Burghes, L., Clarke, L. and Cronin, N. (1997) 'Fathers and Fatherhood in Britain' Occasional Paper no. 23 (London: Family Policy Studies Centre and the Joseph Rowntree Foundation).

Byng-Hall, J. (1995) *Re-writing Family Scripts. Improvisation and Systems Change* (London: Guildford Press).

Camara, K.A. and Resnick, G. (1988) 'Interparental Conflict and Co-operation: Factors Moderating Children's Post-divorce Adjustment', in E.M. Hetherington and J. Arasteh (eds), *Impact of Divorce, Single Parenting and Stepparenting on Children* (Lawrence Erlbaum Associates, Hillsdale, New Jersey, Hove and London), pp. 169–95.

Caspi, A. and Elder, G.H. (1988) 'Emergent Family Patterns: The Intergenerational Construction of Problem Behaviour and Relationships', in R.A. Hinde and J. Stevenson-Hinde (eds), *Relationships within Families: Mutual Influences* (Oxford: Oxford Scientific Publications).

Children Act 1989 (London: HMSO).

Cockett, M. and Tripp, J. (1994) *The Exeter Family Study, Family Breakdown and its Impact on Children* (Joseph Rowntree Foundation, University of Exeter Press).

Cowen, E.J., Pedro Carroll, J.L. and Alpert Gillis, L.J. (1990) 'Relationship Between Support and Adjustment among Children of Divorce', *Journal of Child Psychology and Psychiatry*, Vol. 31, pp. 727–35.

Cox, K.M. and Desforges, M. (1987) *Divorce and the School* (London: Methuen).

Deys, C., Dowling, E. and Golding, V. (1989) 'Clinical Psychology: A Consultative Approach in General Practice', *Journal of the Royal College of General Practitioners*, Vol. 39, pp. 342–44.

Dowling, E. (1993) 'Are Family Therapists Listening to the Young? A Psychological Perspective', *Journal of Family Therapy*, Vol. 15, pp. 403–11.

Dowling, E. (1994) 'Closing the Gap: Consulting in a General Practice', in C. Huffington and H. Brunning (eds), *Internal Consultancy in the Public Sector* (London: Karnac).

Dowling, E. (1998) 'The Systemic Practitioner in General Practice', *Thinking Families, Context*, Vol. 38, p. 4.

Dowling, E. and Osborne, E. (1994) *The Family and the School – A Joint Systems Approach to Problems with Children*, 2nd edn (London: Routledge).

Dowling, E. and Gorell Barnes, G. (1999) 'Children of Divorcing Families: A Clinical Perspective', *Clinical Child Psychology and Psychiatry*, Vol. 4(1), pp. 39–50.

Dowling, J.R. (1980) 'Adjustment from Primary to Secondary School: A One Year Follow-Up', *British Journal of Educational Psychology*, Vol. 50, pp. 26–32.

Dowling, J. (1986) 'Predicting Adjustment after Transfer to Secondary School', in M.B. Youngman (ed.), *Mid Schooling Transfer: Problems and Proposals* (Windsor, Berkshire National Foundation for Educational Research, Nelson).

Dunn, J., Deater-Deckard, K., Pickering, K., O'Connor, T.G. and Golding, J. (1999) 'Child Adjustment and Prosocial Behaviour in Step, Single Parent and Non-Stepfamily Setting: Findings from a Community Study', *Journal of Child Psychology and Psychiatry* (1999 in press).

Elliott, J. and Richards, M.P.M. (1992) 'Children and Divorce: Educational Performance and Behaviour before and after Parental Separation', in *International Journal of Law and The Family*, Vol. 5, pp. 258–76.

Emde, R.N. (1988) 'The Effect of Relationships on Relationships: Developmental Approach to Clinical Intervention', in R.A. Hinde and J. Stevenson-Hinde (eds), *Relationships within Families: Mutual Influences* (Oxford: Oxford Scientific Publications).

Emery, R. and Forehand, R. (1994) 'Parental Divorce and Childrens Well-being: A Focus on Resilience', in R. Haggerty, L. Sherrod, N. Garmezy and M. Rutter (eds), *Stress, Risk and Resilience in Children and Adolescents; Processes, Mechanisms and Interventions* (Cambridge: Cambridge University Press), pp. 64–9.

Family Law Act 1996 (London: HMSO).

Fergusson, D.M., Lynskey, M.T. and Horwood, L.J. (1994) 'The Effects of Parental Separation: The Timing of Separation and Gender on Children's Performance on Cognitive Tests', *Journal of Child Psychology and Psychiatry*, Vol. 35, no. 6, pp. 1077–92.

Fonagy, P., Steele, M., Steele, H., Higgitt, A. and Target, M. (1994) 'The Theory and Practice of Resilience', *Journal of Child Psychology and Psychiatry*, Vol. 35(2), pp. 231–57.

Frieman, B. (1993) 'Separation and Divorce: Children Want their Teachers to Know. Meeting Emotional Needs of Primary and Pre-school Children', *Young Children*, Vol. 48, pp. 58–63.

Fuggle, P., Haydon, K., Hartley, J., Fernandez, K. and Crawford, S. (1998) 'Report on a Pilot Project for the Screening and Treatment of Postnatal Depression in Camden and Islington', unpublished report, Fulham Community Safety programme.

Furstenberg, F.F. (1988) 'Child Care after Divorce and Remarriage', in E.M. Hetherington and J.D. Arasteh (eds), *Impact on Divorce, Single Parenting and Stepparenting on Children* (Hillsdale, N.J.: Lawrence Erlbaum Associates).

Furstenberg, F.F., Morgan, S.P. and Allison, P.D. (1987) 'Paternal Participation and Children's Well-being after Marital Dissolution', *American Sociological Review*, Vol. 52, pp. 695–701.

Garmezy, N. (1991) 'Resilience and Children's Adaptation to Negative Life Events and Stressed Environments', *Paediatric Annals*, Vol. 20, pp. 459–66.

Gelles, R. (1987) *Family Violence*, 2nd edn (London: Sage).

Gorell Barnes, G. (1978) 'Infant Needs and Angry Responses: A Look at Violence in the Family,' in S. Walrond Skinner (ed.), *Family and Marital Psychotherapy: A Critical Approach* (London: Routledge & Kegan Paul).

Gorell Barnes, G. (1991) 'Ambiguities in Post-divorce Relationships', *Journal of Social Work Practice*, Vol. 5(2), pp. 143–50.,

Gorell Barnes, G. (1998) *Family Therapy in Changing Times* (Basingstoke: Macmillan).

Gorell Barnes, G. and Bratley, M. (2000) '*Living Apart but Growing Together: What Helps Fathers Maintain Parenting Relationships with their Children Following Separation and Divorce*' (forthcoming).

Gorell Barnes, G. and Dowling, E. (1997) 'Rewriting the Story: Children, Parents and Post-divorce Narratives', in R.K. Papadopoulos and J. Byng Hall, (eds), *Multiple Voices: Narrative in Systemic Family Psychotherapy* (London: Duckworth, Tavistock Clinic Series).

Gorell Barnes, G. and Henesy, S. (1994) 'Re-claiming a Female Mind from the Experience of Sexual Abuse,' in C. Burck and B. Speed (eds), *Gender, Power and Relationships* (London: Routledge).

Gorell Barnes, G. with Prestige Health Productions (1997) *You're Both Still my Parents*, video (London: W.H. Smith).

Gorell Barnes, G., Thompson, P., Daniel, G. and Burchardt, N. (1998) *Growing up in stepfamilies* (Oxford: Oxford University Press).

Grych, J.H. and Fincham, F.D. (1993) 'Children's Appraisals of Marital Conflict: Initial Investigations of the Cognitive Contextual Framework,' in *Child Development*, Vol. 64, pp. 215–30.

Haliday, E. (1993) *The National Association of Child Contact Centres*, Goldsmith Street, Nottingham, NG1 5UT.

Hall, V. (1997) '*Domestic Violence and Contact*', *Family Law*, December, pp. 813–20.

Hart, B. (1994) '*Gender Role Self-perceptions and Attitudes of Single Fathers: Implications for the Feminist Dialogues in Systemic Theory*, MSc dissertation, London, Tavistock Clinic/Brunel University.

Haskey, J. (1993) 'Divorces in England and Wales', *Population Trends*, Vol. 74 (London: OPCS/HMSO).

Haskey, J. (1994) 'Stepfamilies and Stepchildren in Great Britain', *Population Trends*, Vol. 76 (London: OPCS/HMSO).

Hester, M. and Radford, L. (1996) *Domestic Violence and Child Contact Arrangements in England and Denmark* (Bristol: The Polity Press).

Hetherington, E.M. (1989a) 'Coping with Family Transitions: Winners, Losers and Survivors', *Child Development*, Vol. 60, pp. 1–4.

Hetherington, E.M. (1989b) 'Marital Transitions: A Child's Perspective', *American Psychologist*, Vol. 44(2), pp. 303–12.

Hetherington, E.M. (1992) 'The Role of Individual Difference and Family Relationships in Children's Coping with Divorce and Re-marriage', in P.A. Cowan and E.M. Hetherington (eds), *Family Transitions* (Hillsdale, N.J.: Lawrence Erlbaum Associates), pp. 165–94.

Hetherington, E.M. (1993) 'An Overview of the Virginia Longitudinal Study of Divorce and Remarriage with a Focus on Early Adolescence', *Journal of Family Psychology*, Vol. 7, pp. 79–98.

Hetherington, E.M., Cox, M. and Cox, R. (1979) 'Play and Social Inter-action in Children Following Divorce', *Journal of Social Issues*, Vol. 35, pp. 26–49.

Hetherington, E.M. and Stanley-Hagan, M. (1997) 'Parenting in Divorced and Remarried Families', in M.H. Bernstein (ed.), *Handbook of Parenting* (Hillsdale, N.J.: Lawrence Erlbaum Associates).

Hetherington, E. and Tryon, A.S. (1989) 'His and Hers Divorce', *The Family Therapy Networker*, November, pp. 1–16.

Hill, P. (1989) *Adolescent Psychiatry* (Edinburgh: Churchill Living-stone).

Isaacs, M.B., Leon, G. and Donahue, A.M. (1987) 'Who are the "Normal" Children of Divorce? On the Need to Specify a Population', *Journal of Divorce*, pp. 107–19.

Isaacs, M. (1988) 'The Visitation Schedule and Child Adjustment. A Three Year Study', *Family Process*, Vol. 27, pp. 251–6.

Jeffreys, P. (1998) *Family Court Welfare*, London, personal communications.

Jenkins, J., Smith. M. and Graham, P. (1988) 'Coping with Parental Quar-rels', *Journal of American Academy of Child and Adolescent Psychiatry*, Vol. 28, pp. 182–9.

Jenkins, J.M. and Smith, M. (1990) 'Factors Protecting Children Living in Disharmonious Homes', *Journal of the American Academy of Child and Adolescent Psychiatry*, Vol. 29, pp. 60–9.

Jones, G. (1995) *Family Support for Young People* (London: Family Policy Studies Centre).

Kelly, L. (1998) 'Current Research on Children's Post-divorce Adjust-ment', *Family and Conciliation Courts Review*, Vol. 31, pp. 29–49.

Kidscape (1998) 'Keeping Children Safe', 152 Buckingham Road, London SW1.

Kiecolt Glaser, J.K., Fischer, B.S., Ogrocki, P., Stout, J., Speicher, C. and Gla-ser, R. (1987) 'Marital Quality, Marital Disruption and Immune Func-tion', *Psychosomatic Medicine*, Vol. 49, pp. 13–33.

Kier, C. and Lewis, C. (1998) 'Pre-school Sibling Interaction in Sepa-rated and Married Families: Are Same Sex Pairs or Older Sisters more Sociable?' *Journal of Child Psychology and Psychiatry*, Vol. 39, pp. 191–201.

Kiernan, K.E. (1992) 'The Impact of Family Disruption in Childhood on Transitions made in Young Adult life', *Population Studies*, Vol. 46, pp. 213–34.

Kiernan, K. and Estaugh, V. (1993) 'Cohabitation. Extra Marital Childbear-ing and Social Policy', Occasional Paper no.17 (London: Family Policy Studies Centre).

Kitson, G.C. and Holmes, W.M. (1992) *Portrait of Divorce: Adjustment to Marital Breakdown* (New York: Guilford).

Kraemer, S. (1995) 'What are Fathers for?', in C. Burck and B. Speed (eds), *Gender, Power and Relationships* (London: Routledge).

Kruk, E. (1992) 'Psychological and Structural Factors Contributing to the Disengagement of Non-Custodial Fathers after Divorce', *Family and Conciliation Courts Review*, Vol. 30 (1), pp. 81–101.

Lamb, M.E., Frodi, A.M., Hwang, C.P., Frodi, M. and Steinberg, J. (1982) 'Mother and Father Interaction Involving Play and Holding in Traditional and not-traditional Swedish Families', *Developmental Psychology*, Vol. 18, pp. 215–21.

Lamb, M.E. (1997) *The Role of the Father in Child Development*, 3rd edn (New York: John Wiley).

Lund, M. (1987) 'The Non-custodial Father: Common Challenges in Parenting after Divorce', in M. O'Brien (ed.), *Re-assessing Fatherhood: New Observations on Fathers of the Modern Family* (London: Sage).

McLanahan, S.S. and Booth, K. (1989) 'Mother-only Families: Problems, Prospects and Policies', *Journal of Marriage and the Family*, Vol. 51, pp. 557–80.

McLanahan, S.S. and Sandefur, G. (1994) *Growing up with a Single Parent* (Cambridge, Mass: Harvard University Press).

McNab, S. (1993) 'Latency-age Children's Adjustment to Parental Separation: Gender Differences, Home School Relationships and Pupil-Teacher Attachments', MSc dissertation, London, Tavistock Clinic/Brunel University.

Maccoby, E.E. (1986) 'Social Groupings in Childhood: Their Relationship to Prosocial and Antisocial Behaviour in Boys and Girls', in D. Olweus, J. Block and M. Radke Yarrow (eds), *Development of Prosocial and Antisocial Behaviour in Boys and Girls: Research Theories and Issues'* (New York: Academic Press), pp. 263–4.

Maccoby, E.E., Depner, C.E. and Mnookin, R.H. (1990) 'Co-parenting in the Second Year after Divorce', *Journal of Marriage and the Family*, Vol. 52, pp. 141–55.

Maccoby, E. and Mnookin, R.H. (1992) *Dividing the Child: Social and Legal Dilemmas of Custody* (Cambridge, Mass: Harvard University Press).

Maccoby, E.E., Buchanan, C.M., Mnookin, R.H. and Dornbusch, S.M (1993) 'Post-divorce Roles of Mothers and Fathers in the Lives of their Children', *Journal of Family Psychology*, Vol. 7, pp. 1–15.

Main, M. (1992) 'Metacognitive Knowledge, Metacognitive Monitoring and Singular (coherent) vs. Multiple (incoherent) Models of Attachment. Findings and Directions for Further Research', in C. Murray Parkes, J. Stevenson-Hinde and P. Marris (eds), *Attachment across the life cycle* (London:Routledge).

Main, M., Kaplan, N. and Cassidy, J. (1985) 'Security in Infancy, Childhood and Adulthood: A Move to the Level of Representation', in I. Bretherton and E. Waters (eds), *Growing Points of Attachment – Theory and Research. Monographs of the Society for Research in Child Development*, serial no. 209, Vol. 50, nos. 1–2.

Mitchell, A. (1985) *Children in the Middle: Living Through Divorce* (London: Tavistock).

Moffitt, T.E. and Caspi, A. (1998) 'Annotation. Implications of Violence between Intimate Partners for Child Psychologists and Psychiatrists', *Journal of Child Psychology and Psychiatry*, Vol. 39, no. 2, pp. 137–44.

Ochiltree, G. (1990) *Children in Stepfamilies* (Sydney: Prentice Hall).

Parke, R.D. and Tinsley, B.R. (1981) 'The Father's Role in Infancy: Determinants of Involvement in Caregiving and Play', in M.E. Lamb (ed.),

The Role of the Father in Child Development, 2nd edn (New York: John Wiley).

Pecherek, A. (1996) 'Growing up in Non-nuclear Families', in A. Sigston *et al.* (eds), *Psychology in Practice* (David Fulton Publishers).

Richards, M.P.M. (1991) 'The Effects of Parental Divorce on Children', *Archives of Diseases in Childhood*, Vol. 66, pp. 915–16.

Richards, M.P.M. (1995) 'The International Year of the Family – Family Research', *The Psychologist*, January, pp. 17–20.

Roberts, J. (1995) 'Lone Mothers and their Children, *British Journal of Psychiatry*, Vol. 167, pp. 159–62.

Robinson, M. (1997) *Divorce as Family Transition* (London: Karnac).

Rodgers, B. and Pryor, J. (1998) *Divorce and Separation. The Outcomes for Children* (York: Joseph Rowntree Foundation).

Rose, M.K. (1992) 'Elective Single Mothers and their Children: the Missing Fathers', *Child and Adolescent Social Work*, Vol. 9, pp. 21–3.

Rutter, M. (1966) *Children of Sick Parents: An Environmental and Psychiatric Study*, Maudsley Monograph, no. 16 (London: Oxford University Press).

Rutter, M. (1987) 'Psychosocial Resilience and Protective Mechanisms', in S. Rolf, A. Masten, D. Cicchetti, D. Nuechterlein and S. Weintraub (eds), *Risk and Protective Factors in the Development of Psychopathology* (New York: Cambridge University Press).

Rutter, M. (1987) 'Psychosocial Resilience and Protective Mechanisms', *American Journal of Orthopsychiatry*, Vol. 57, pp. 316–31.

Rutter, M. (1999) 'Resilience Concepts and Findings: Implications for Family Therapy', *Journal of Family Therapy* (forthcoming).

Schlosser, A. and De'Ath, E. (1995) 'Looked after Children and their Families', F 2, Stepfamily Association UK.

Seltzer, J.A. (1991) 'Relationships between Fathers and Children who Live Apart. The Father's Role after Separation', *Journal of Marriage and the Family*, Vol. 53, pp. 79–101.

Seltzer, J.A. and Brandreth, Y. (1994) 'What Fathers Say about Involvement with Children after Separation', *Journal of Family Issues*, Vol. 15, pp. 49–77.

Shaw, D. and Emery, R. (1987) 'Parental Conflict and Other Correlates of the Adjustment of School-age Children whose Parents have Separated', *Journal of Abnormal Child Psychology*, Vol. 15, pp. 269–81.

Simons, R.L. and associates (1996) *Understanding Differences between Divorced and Intact Families – Stress, Interaction and Child Outcome* (London: Sage), Understanding Family Series.

Simpson, B. (1994) 'Access and Child Contact Centres in England and Wales: An Ethnographic Perspective', *Children and Society*, Vol. 8, pp. 42–5.

Simpson, B., McCarthy, P. and Walker. J. (1995) *Being There : Fathers after Divorce* (Newcastle: Relate Centre for Family Studies).

Sroufe, L.A. and Fleeson, J. (1988) 'The Coherence of Family Relationships', in R.A. Hinde and Stevenson-Hinde (eds), *Relationships Within Families: Mutual Influence* (Oxford: Oxford Scientific Publications).

Stacey, J. (1993) 'Good Riddance to "the Family": A Response to David Popenoe', *Journal of Marriage and the Family*, Vol. 55, pp. 545–7.

Stanley, N. (1997) 'Domestic Violence and Child Abuse: Developing Social Work Practice', *Child and Family Social Work*, Vol. 2, pp. 135–45.

Tasker, F.L. and Golumbok, S. (1997) *Growing Up in a Lesbian Family* (New York: Guildford Press).

Wadsby, M. (1993) 'Children of Divorce and their Parents,' in Linkoping *University Medical Dissertations* no 405 (Linkoping Department of Child and Adolescent Psychiatry, Faculty of Health Sciences, Linkoping University s.58185, Sweden).

Walczack, Y. and Burns, S. (1984) *Divorce: The Child's Point of View* (London: Harper & Row).

Walker, R. (1997) 'What are the Differences in Both Beliefs and Behaviours of Fathers in Relation to their Non-resident Children and their Stepchildren?', MSc dissertation, London, Tavistock Clinic/Brunel University.

Wallerstein, J.S. (1985) 'The Overburdened Child: Some Long-term Consequences of Divorce', *American Journal of Social Work*, March/April.

Wallerstein, J.S. and Kelly, J.B. (1980) *Surviving the Breakup: How children and Parents cope with Divorce* (New York: Basic Books).

Wallerstein, J.S. (1991) 'The Long-term Effects of Divorce on Children – a Review', *Journal of the American Academy of Child and Adolescent Psychiatry*, Vol. 30, pp. 349–60.

West Midland Police HQ Family Protection Unit 0121 626 5092.

Wren, B. (1997) *'Mothering a Daughter in Father's Absence'*, MSc dissertation, London, Tavistock Clinic/Brunel University.

Youngman, M.B. (ed.) (1986) *Mid-Schooling Transfer: Problems and Proposals* (Windsor, Berks: National Foundation for Educational Research, Nelson).

INDEX